RUSSIA UNDER THREE TSARS

Dr. Michael N. Kalantar

With an Introduction by Irene Vartanoff
Appendix: An interview with Leo Tolstoy

Cover design by BookGraphics.net
Formatting by Polgarus Studio

Published by Irene Vartanoff
www.irenevartanoff.com
P.O. Box 27
Gerrardstown, WV 25420

ISBN 978-0-9861252-8-7 (ebook)
ISBN 978-0-9861252-9-4 (print)

RUSSIA UNDER THREE TSARS

Contents

INTRODUCTION

An eyewitness to history, Dr. Michael N. Kalantar experienced the Russian Revolution firsthand. He also had exclusive access to the original manuscript memoirs of his uncle, Mikhail Tarielovich, Count Loris-Melikov, who had been the reform minister to Tsar Alexander II. This book is Kalantar's account of the origins of the Russian Revolution from the perspective of an unabashed tsarist and insider. During the critical years immediately prior to the revolution of 1917, Kalantar held the post of secretary-in-chief of the Imperial Senate (the Duma), among others. He later served as a judge during the doomed warfare against the conquering Red Army.

Kalantar recounts how the last three tsars, Alexander II, Alexander III, and Nicholas II, attempted to forestall the forces of revolution over the period of 1881 to 1911. The Russian Revolution happened anyway. Unfortunately, the final portion of Kalantar's manuscript, the part intimately describing the events of the Revolution, has been lost. Thus this book does not tell the events of the Revolution itself. Incomplete as this account currently is, it is still a valuable, previously unpublished part of the historical record.

Eyewitness accounts of history are always subject to bias, and in this case the bias is welcome, as it honestly elucidates the attitudes of the elites at a time of great civil and political unrest. History written from the perspective of another century is no less biased. Kalantar does not bother to speak with total objectivity about the people whom he considers to have been in error, or for that matter outright scoundrels. This lack of evenhandedness is a plus rather than a minus. The man who knew the personalities of the major actors on the historical stage does us all a favor by telling us of their flaws as he perceives them rather than by bending over backwards to pretend that they had none. No historian alive today knew Tsar Nicholas II or the Russian court or the Russian political scene as Kalantar did. In his position in the Duma, Kalantar played a key role in a transition government that was overtaken by the extremism of the Bolsheviks. He gives us his opinion and his knowledge of the events leading up to the Russian Revolution, always from his perspective as a member of the tsarist establishment, and as a working member of the doomed political movement that sought to change the government of the Russian empire for the better while retaining the Tsar as the head of state.

None therefore have as much right to their opinions as Kalantar does. He tells the story of the last tsars of Russia, having been on the spot or gotten the particulars directly from the people who were there when the events occurred. As with most histories of one's own national tragedy, he knows the details, details that we Westerners often never learn. This intimate account gives us information that reflects only what was known at the time and shortly after. Such information is valuable because whatever was publicly or privately known contemporaneously was what shaped public and private opinion and activity at the time.

Michael N. Kalantar (1883–1958) was born in Yerevan, in the southern part of the old Russian empire, and related by blood or marriage to many Georgian-Armenian noble houses. Kalantar obtained his first degree from the University of St. Petersburg, and his second as doctor of laws from Heidelberg University, which published his doctoral thesis in 1903. He also studied at the Sorbonne before returning to Russia and beginning his political and judicial career.

During this period, Kalantar visited Leo Tolstoy at his estate. Much later, Kalantar wrote an article about the political import of their meeting, which is included as an Appendix.

Kalantar's scholarly and political career was interrupted by the Russian Revolution. Once there was no more Tsar to fight for, and the army battles were over, many tsarists tried to accommodate themselves to the new Bolshevik regime. Those of noble birth or of substantial education often found they were deliberately pilloried by the Soviet government in an effort to blame its own failures on the remnants of the old Russian society. Former aristocrats were increasingly persecuted. In 1923, Kalantar and his wife left Russia for Constantinople, where he became a news correspondent and translator. A few years later, they moved to Athens, Greece. Kalantar immigrated alone to the United States in 1930, becoming a naturalized citizen in 1937. During and after

World War II, he worked for the U.S. Army Map Service as a translator, having mastered many languages, including but not limited to Georgian, Russian, German, French, modern Greek, and English.

Under the various spellings of his name, including Kalantaroff and Kalantarov, Kalantar wrote political articles for Russian language newspapers. He composed other articles in English for a variety of publications including *American Slav* magazine, and was a frequent contributor to the *Washington Star* newspaper. This book is entirely in his words, written by him in English, not a translation, and not edited to change word choices. I have modernized only some punctuation and standardized a very few proper name usages to American styles.

Dr. Kalantar, as my parents always referred to him, died in 1958, leaving behind the manuscript of this book. He had tried in vain to interest American publishers in it during his last years, thus any references to "today" refer to the world political tensions and the fraught situation of the Red Scare and the Cold War that existed in the 1950s in the U.S. This literary effort would seem to have died with him. For over fifty years, his manuscript was in my family's possession, as my father was his cousin and closest surviving relative. Finally the digital age has made it possible to publish this story without changing it to follow the fashions of a particular era. I now can disseminate this manuscript to any and all who may be interested in a scholar's true historical account of the Russian Revolution.

Dr. Kalantar was also my godfather. When I was a little girl, he was an elderly man who generously gave me Madame

Alexander dolls and sterling silver spoons. I am happy to give back to him now, and add to the store of eyewitness historical documents about the Russian Revolution.

Irene Vartanoff
West Virginia

Chapter 1
ONE DAY THAT CHANGED THE WORLD

The world today is in the throes of an acute crisis. It faces a grandiose, difficult task—resolve this crisis and point out to mankind the path it is to follow.

The Russian Revolution happens to be the major underlying cause of this crisis. The fate of the rest of the world is tightly bound to the fate of Russia and, alas, cannot be severed from it. The Russian Revolution has shaken the edifice of Christian culture which was built by past generations, and in its gigantic scope has torn the world from its natural state and thrown it into an unending series of upheavals, struggles, disasters.

Where then are the sources, the original causes of this ominous historical event? We must find these sources, subject them to the deepest analysis, or else we will never be able to understand the complex events of our time.

The great Russian Revolution began not in February 1917,

as it is commonly believed, but on 1 March 1881.

On that day was heard the first clap of thunder in the terrible storm that thirty-six years later was to sweep away a mighty Empire.

On 1 March 1881, in the very center of that Empire's capital, its ruler, Emperor Alexander II, was killed by a terrorist's bomb and, following the inflexible law of succession, his son, Alexander III ascended the throne.

History is fond of contrasts. The human mind is powerless to fathom the mute language of its symbols.

Never before had the throne of all Russias been occupied by a monarch of such chivalrous kindness, such enlightened mind and such iron will as was Alexander II. His reforms were more profound, farther reaching and more substantial than those of Peter the Great.

It was he who, with one stroke of his pen, put an end to serfdom, giving freedom and land to more than 23 million peasants-serfs. With this act Alexander II split Russian history into two irreconcilable halves, on one hand smothering serfdom with all its savage cruelties in the night of past ages, opening, on the other, the gates of a free life for future generations. Quite justly did the celebrated writer Zhukovski suggest that a new Russian calendar begin its reckoning from the day of liberation of the serfs.

It was Alexander II who instituted free courts, the jury system, equalized all citizens before the law, abolished corporeal punishment, created city and provincial self-governments.

Science, literature, music, the press were lifted to their

rightful levels of significance and burst forth with such names as Dostoyevsky, Tolstoy, Tchaikovsky, Mendeleev.

It was he, finally, who listened to the voice of the people and to the wise counseling of his Minister Count Loris-Melikov and agreed to take still another step in his trail-blazing with the introduction of constitutional government and the granting of a parliamentary charter.

"I am ready now and here," he said to Count Loris-Melikov, "to sign the broadest constitution if only I can be completely convinced that this would bring happiness to my people." The Minister was able to dispel the last remaining doubts and Alexander II set 1 March as the date for the signing of the charter. Russia was being led out onto the broad avenue of its natural development.

Sunday, 1 March 1881. Every slightest detail of this day, so indelibly etched in the minds of contemporaries, has direct bearing on the history of a great nation, on a centuries-old dynasty standing at the turning point of its fate. It is a day like all other winter days in St. Petersburg, gray and snowy, and the streets are alive with the stir of a Sunday crowd. At the huge Mikhailovsky Armory preparations are being completed for the traditional review of the Guards by the Emperor. Such reviews, occasions of pomp and pageantry attended by the top military hierarchies, the diplomatic corps and a glittering society, were supposed to take place every Sunday. And yet now, for several Sundays in a row it had been announced that the Emperor would not attend and the reviews had been cancelled. Rumors of possible ill health on the part of the Monarch were rampant in the capital. On this Sunday, however, 1 March, all doubts are dispelled—the review will take place, Alexander will be there.

In the Winter Palace all is in order. The Emperor arises some fifteen minutes earlier than his accustomed hour. As usual he takes his favorite walk through the immense halls of the palace. He is in an excellent mood. With impatience he awaits the arrival of his favorite Minister, Count Loris-Melikov. The Tsar remembers well his decision for this day and once a decision is taken, Alexander II dislikes to put off its execution.

9:30 a.m. Loris-Melikov arrives at the palace and is immediately received by the Emperor. His face looks worried, exhausted. With barely any introduction he begs the Tsar to cancel the review at the Armory. The police have definite information that an attempt at the Emperor's life has been planned for this day. In fact, they have already arrested Zhelyabov, one of the principal Nihilist leaders.

"So much the better," interrupts the Tsar. "If the leader is arrested, I can go on with my plans. I am going to the review. I do not wish for my people to judge me a coward."

The Count makes further attempts to change Alexander's mind. To no avail.

"Better show me the documents which you, Count, have in your briefcase," exclaims the Emperor smiling. "The Charter!"

Yes, this is the Constitutional Charter in its final form, the very Charter that was to give the Russian people a representative government, a document other peoples of Europe had been able to obtain only after prolonged and bloody struggles.

The Emperor reads the Charter with concentrated attention. At the bottom of it he sees the signature of his son, Crown Prince Alexander. To make the document even more firmly valid, the farsighted Minister had already secured that signature on the previous day. The Emperor smiles. Then he picks up a pen and affixes his signature in a sprawling hand.

"No later than tomorrow morning," he orders, "make this document public."

With a certain haste Alexander II retires to the inner chambers of the palace. He wants to tell his wife, Yekaterina Yurievskaya (after the death of his wife, the Empress Maria Alexsandrovna, Alexander II married Princess Yurievskaya morganatically, according to the rites of the Russian Orthodox Church), about what he has just done.

"How happy I am!" cries the Princess.

"I am even afraid of my happiness," the Monarch answers "I've done for my people all that was in my power to do."

And truly, what else could Emperor Alexander II do for the good of his people? Live. Live at least through the following day, live to see his manifesto made public and valid. According to the statutes of the Russian Empire a law or an Imperial Manifesto became valid only after its publication. Thus an act signed by the Monarch, but not as yet officially made public, in no way constituted a law.

Meanwhile Loris-Melikov does not leave the palace. He is well aware of and perhaps even has a premonition about the impending danger. He goes to see Princess Yurievskaya, willing to gamble on her well-known influence upon her crowned consort. Perhaps the tears and entreaties of a woman will be more effective than the reasoning of a Minister? Seemingly the gamble pays off. Alexander agrees to cancel the review. His life is saved!

Or is it? Luck is seldom on the side of those who hesitate in making decisions.

Loris-Melikov has scarcely left the palace when another visitor is announced: Grand Duchess Alexandra Iosifovna, the Emperor's sister-in-law and a great favorite of the Monarch. Was this visit a blind, cruel trick of fate or was the Grand Duchess the unwitting tool of a conspirator, sent forth once again to change Alexander's mind? History will never know. In the course of conversation Alexandra Iosifovna mentions the fact, quite casually it would seem, that her youngest nephew, Dimitri, has been named to convey the salute of the Guards to their Emperor during the review. She stresses how very proud and greatly elated the young man feels at the chance of presenting himself to his beloved Sovereign. Alexander is impressed, his sense of chivalry aroused. "I am going to the review," he declares. "Countermand my previous order."

These words sealed the fate of the Emperor and of his people.

At 12:45 the court carriage is at the door of the Winter Palace, the Escort detachment of Cossacks around it. Frol Sergeiev, the coachman universally known for his enormous beard, is on the box. Alexander likes his coachman and greets him cordially. Then he orders, "To the Armory, via the Pevchenski bridge." This is a slight change from the habitual route, dictated perhaps by thought of caution.

One p.m. Loud hurrahs greet the entry of the Emperor,

mounted on a beautiful black stallion, into the Armory. His son, the heir to the throne, is already there, stationed at his appointed position on the right flank of the Battalion. Having graciously acknowledged the ovation, the Emperor receives the reports of the officers of the day, conveying the salute of the troops. Among these is his nephew, young Grand Duke Dimitri, the actual cause of the Emperor's presence at the Armory. The Tsar returns the salute of the Guards. The view takes place. It lasts almost until three o'clock.

Two forty-five p.m. The Imperial carriage leaves the Armory on its way back to the palace, followed by a sleigh bearing the Chief of Police, Colonel Dvorzhinsky and "Okhrana" Captain Kulebiakin. Swiftly it glides on the snow, surrounded by the Escort Cossacks. It turns onto the quay of the Ekaterinensky Canal. An explosion is heard. A cannon shot? But it seems to have come from under the Emperor's sleigh. Who is shooting, and why?.... It is a slight young man with long blond hair, standing on the quay. He has hurled a small, innocent bundle against the sleigh. But the bundle is a homemade bomb.

Dense smoke envelops the scene. Then, slowly, it disperses in the breeze, revealing a ghastly picture—the Tsar's carriage is damaged, two Escort Cossacks and a passer-by, a baker's apprentice, lie on the ground, bloody and dying.

Cool and resourceful, the coachman does not stop. Get the Emperor to the palace is his only thought and he controls the panicked horses and whips them on. But the Tsar himself orders him to stop. He wants to survey the scene of the disaster. Calmly, with a firm step and ignoring the entreaties of the Chief of Police, he alights from the carriage and walks back.

"Fool! What have you done?" he exclaims confronting the assassin, Rysakov, already in the clutches of the crowd that is ready to tear him to pieces.

"Don't touch me, don't beat me," screams Rysakov.

"Russians! Miserable, benighted people!"

"Where is the Tsar? Is he safe?" Somebody in the crowd, confused, has not recognized the Monarch.

"Thank God, I was spared. But here… look…." He kneels over the agonized baker's apprentice and blesses him with the sign of the cross.

"It's too early to thank God," screams Rysakov in answer, furiously, yet triumphantly. He knows that more renegades like himself are in the crowd, waiting. Like himself they were organized and sent forth at the last moment by the revolutionary Sonia Perovskaya who had assumed leadership of the plot after Zhelyabov's arrest.

Alexander moves away. He takes a few steps. His eyes meet the eyes of a man, the only man in the crowd who has not taken off his hat. They are face to face. The man lifts his arms and with all his strength hurls a white bundle at the legs of the Monarch. A second deafening explosion. Smoke, snow, shapeless, horrible shreds, unrecognizable as parts of human bodies. Wounded and dying people all around. In the midst of them…. Emperor Alexander II, the Tsar Liberator, half-lying, clutching the iron grille of the canal. His face is covered with blood, his cap and coat are in tatters, his legs mangled up to the knees. Before the Monarch in much the same condition lies the assassin.

"Is the heir alive? murmurs the Tsar. He wants to cross himself, but his hand does not obey him. "It is cold... cold...." he keeps repeating. And then, "To the palace. Take me to the palace.... That's where I want to die...."

Gently, carefully a dozen hands lift him and carry him to the sleigh. Those are not the hands of servile courtiers. Those are the people, horrified, grieving, yet even now unaware of the full significance of what has taken place before their eyes.

Twice during the trip to the palace, in a faint but insistent voice, Alexander asks his faithful subject and servant Captain Kulebiakin who, wounded, is seated next to him in the sleigh: "And you, Kulebiakin, are you hurt?" The bitter, inconsolable tears of the gravely injured man are his answer.

The Palace Square is filled with people. The huge crowd, silent, as if in a stupor, waits. At 3:35 p.m. the Imperial Standard atop the Palace, signifying the presence there of a member of the Royal family is slowly, mournfully lowered. The crowd in the square, the Russian people, understand that it is all over. The great Tsar Liberator is dead.

In absolute monarchies the law of succession is ironclad— the eldest living son inherits the throne of the father. This law admits no choice, no criticism of the candidate. Thus it has always been and thus it must happen now. A new Emperor, Alexander III, makes his immediate entrance onto the vast arena of Russian history. Thirty-six years old, bearded, tall, athletically built, a soldier and an honorable man, he is not, however, of a statesman's caliber. Yet he becomes the master of the Russian people's destinies.

Truly awesome and fateful for Russia is this day of March the 1st. And it is not over yet.

Inside the Winter Palace doctors and servants are hastily completing their mournful task. The room in which Alexander II died is ready, the furniture has been removed. On a simple iron bed, his campaign cot in the Turkish expedition, lies the Tsar. The expression on his face is serene. He died conscious of duty fulfilled. No ornaments. In accordance with the deceased Monarch's will the crown and all Imperial regalia are missing.

The clergy arrives and the first requiem service is under way. The prayers are interrupted by weeping. Even the officiating priests are unable to control their grief. The service is attended by members of the Imperial family and a few among the highest functionaries of the State. Among these is Count Loris-Melikov, closest and most devoted collaborator of the deceased Tsar, key figure in that glorious epoch of the Great Reforms.

What thoughts crowd that statesman's powerful mind before the lifeless body of his Tsar? We can only guess. One thing is certain—better than anyone else does this man understand the deepest, fateful meaning of the change in rulers that has just occurred. Perhaps his keen, unerring eye already sees the awesome events, the flames and blood and horrors that are to engulf his country thirty-six years from now. But the Count performs his duty to the end.

No sooner is the service over that he requests an audience with Alexander III to settle the question that can stand no delay—must he, as was ordered by Alexander II, make public the Constitution Manifesto, thereby introducing in Russia a new representative regime?

"The will of my father is sacred," answers the new Tsar without hesitation. "Publish it no later than tomorrow."

The hours drag by. It is late at night. But March the 1st, 1881 is still not over. Count Loris-Melikov is suddenly awakened by an envoy from the Palace, bearing an express Imperial Order: *Stop the publication of the Manifesto: destroy the copies already printed.*

"The miserable man!" rages the Count. "He has gone back on his own signature."

***

What prompted Tsar Alexander III to change his decision so drastically and in the dead of night? Who could have so decisively, almost magically it seems, influenced the young Emperor? For a long time these questions puzzled all of Russia. And only now does the diary of Count Loris-Melikov, inherited by the writer of this text, lift the pall from this closely-guarded palace mystery.

The answer is Pobedonostsev, once the Tsar's tutor, and a fanatic of the principle of absolute monarchy. On that sleepless night he was at the Monarch's side exerting upon him an extraordinary, fatal influence.

Pobedonostsev is a figure who baffles the historian. Gaunt, clean-shaven, ascetic, with fearless, piercing eyes behind thick glasses, he lived the life of a scholar in his book-filled study where, in one corner, a light constantly burned before a triptych of ancient icons. So far no key has been found to his secretive soul. He seemed bodily to have arisen from the mystical depths of Russian antiquity. His power was not in a dictatorial pose, or dictatorial acts, nor was he driven, it would seem, by personal ambition. Pobedonostsev's power lay in his incredible ability to influence the thoughts and acts of other people while he himself remained in the shadows.

It was to this man that Alexander III sent a letter by special messenger on that fateful night, complaining of the difficulty and gravity of the new political situation and concluding: "I trust in God alone."

Reading this letter, Pobedonostsev with his acute political flair understood that "God alone" was not enough for the young Tsar at that juncture—he also needed a counselor. And Pobedonostsev rushed to the palace forthwith. He brought into play all the power of his extraordinary erudition, of his keen mind and of his eloquence to change Alexander III's mind during that midnight interview. "Only an immediate shift to safeguard the principles of absolute monarchy can save Russia from upheavals and revolution," hammered Pobedonostsev before his former ward, soon convincing him that the only conceivable course of action was to rescind without further delay the order concerning the Constitution Manifesto publication. This was a sharp, fatal break in the destiny of Imperial Russia. The harsh and powerful hand of Alexander III irrevocably turned the wheel of Russian history onto the path of reaction. Where did it lead? Whose political shadows loomed in the sinister shadows of the coming years? The answers to this have already been given by ever impartial time.

The sad news about the terrible death of Alexander II swiftly spread all over Russia, reaching the town of Simbirsk, in Siberia. Here, very late that same night, a teacher of mathematics came to see the Superintendent of city schools, Ilya Nikolayevich Ulianov. He had a worried look on his face and, unbuttoning his overcoat, he said with a frightened voice: "A telegram came from St. Petersburg. Tsar Alexander II was killed by a bomb!...." As he was speaking, the teacher's eyes fell upon Volodia, a small boy with freckles, brown eyes and reddish hair who was doing his homework in a corner of the room. The boy met the teacher's gaze and held it. He pushed aside his books and listened with concentration to all that was said, as if trying to fathom the deep significance of what had happened.

Volodia Ulianov was no one else but the future Lenin, founder of Russian Bolshevism.

On that day all hopes died for a peaceful renovation of the country. Russia was not destined to continue along the broad avenue of progress traced for it by the slain Emperor. Russia was thrown into a historical tangle, into a series of near mystical misunderstandings that lasted for two more reigns and were resolved only by a revolution in the ghastly way revolutions always perform their functions.

***

Is not then history merely a sequence of fortuities? Consider the irony of Alexander's assassination. What a weird coincidence—reaction and extreme radicalism clashing to the death in the smoke and uproar of an exploding bomb!

Had Sofia Perovskaya and her terrorist colleagues thrown leaflets on that fateful day in 1881 instead of bombs, the history of Russia and of the world would have taken a totally different direction.

Chapter 2
ROAD TO REACTION

Alexander III became Emperor of Russia and immediately embraced reaction. Having taken this step, he never recanted, even to his dying hour. On his very deathbed he instructed his son, Nicholas II: "Be sure not to make any concessions, for if you give them a finger, they will bite off the whole hand." Pobedonostsev's rigid doctrine was akin to the intimate feeling within the heart of the Tsar himself.

Alexander III immediately broke off from all the enlightened friends of his father and entrusted power to individuals who knew and shared his own true thoughts. The brilliant Count Loris-Melikov and his talented liberal collaborators Miliutin and Abasa were sent into retirement. The Count was replaced by Count Ignatiev, a hypocrite about whom it has been said that in all his life he never spoke a word of truth. Count Ignatiev had gained notoriety in the East, as ambassador to Constantinople. The peoples of the East do not resent deceit and betrayal, provided these are presented in a pleasant, ingratiating form.

The shattering impression produced by his father's terrible death determined in many ways the future line of conduct of Alexander III. After the execution of the terrorists—a group of fanatics-nihilists—Alexander III threw all the forces of state power into the struggle against revolutionaries and nihilists and against those circles from which the latter mostly came— immature, hot-headed university students. Academic strata on higher levels, such as professors, teachers and all kinds of intellectuals, were also regarded by the monarch with great suspicion.

He took severe measures intended to limit academic freedom on all levels and tightened censorship over the printed word as a whole. Alexander III obviously shared Pobedonostsev's point of view that education is no guarantee of the people's happiness. Once the governor of the Tobolsk region, in a report to the Tsar, sadly mentioned the tremendous incidence of illiteracy in the province under his jurisdiction. Alexander III made a notation: "And thank God for that!"

It is easier, the Tsar probably thought, to govern ignorant than educated citizens. But alas, time was to show that blind slaves can easiest of all be changed into savage rebels.

Basing himself—as did Pobedonostsev—on the tenet that the Orthodox Church is the basis of autocracy, the Tsar showed intolerance towards all other faiths and sects: Moslems, Jews, Catholics, Old Believers, etc. Following a program worked out by Pobedonostsev, Alexander III exerted untiring efforts to strengthen the influence of the legitimate church throughout the country. Numberless new places of worship were built everywhere, in the center of Russia, in the north up to the very polar circle, in the south in the impervious mountains of the Caucasus. The number of new monasteries alone reached 153 during the reign of Alexander III. Students, teachers, civil servants, officers and soldiers were all required by law to go to church and partake of Communion.

At the same time a whole network of parochial schools was organized in the hope that the people would thereby become close to the Church as desired. The number of newly-organized institutions of this type reached 31,592.

The future showed what a sad abyss there turned out to be between the planned program and the achieving of its goal. At the critical time of trouble and catastrophe not a single graduate of these educational centers was able to come forth as leader and peacemaker. Apparently other ways, ideals and methods were needed, far removed from those used by Pobedonostsev.

Meanwhile the life of the Russian people, as it developed in the nineteenth century, was basically far from Godless. In this life faith in God was deeply ingrained and the simple Russian people sought God, harboring thoughts of Him in their hearts. That is why even great Russian geniuses like Tolstoy and Dostoyevsky were deeply religious men. This religious exaltation, however, froze under the influence of Pobedonostsev's Church policies.

Nor did the Church alone feel Alexander's iron reactionary band. All aspects of Russian life were subjected to repression and regressive changes. Local governments, schools, the press, courts of law, civil servants, the army, all had to serve the aims of reaction or be silent, as if nonexistent. Even praise of the reforms of Alexander II was forbidden as a sign of inadmissible liberalism!

The epoch of the reign of Alexander III was indeed the most reactionary period in all of Russian history. What sort of a harvest would eventually come from the seeds of reaction sown by such an inexorable hand throughout the country? Few people thought or worried about that at the time. Count D. Tolstoy, one of the Tsar's ministers, answered a query on the subject in the following characteristic words: "I know, I know! But we are interested in the present. Just let it all last through our own lifetime."

The prediction of the count-minister was correct. Reaction was good for almost a quarter of a century—but no more. The fruits of Alexander's regime were to be reaped by another monarch: his son.

The memory of his father's terrifying death made Alexander III ever aware of the dangers to which he himself was constantly exposed. His entourage, especially the police and security agencies, did all that was in their power to increase this fear, thus furthering more than one personal career.

The Tsar often found threatening letters on his desk, or in the pockets of his clothes. Similar letters began to appear in the pockets of his children's clothes. The idea of seclusion, as sole means of protecting himself from the bombs and bullets of terrorists, was ceaselessly inculcated into the mind of the monarch.

And thus, the capital with all its spacious avenues and

squares became hateful to the Tsar because of the gory memories it evoked and he transferred his residence to Gatchina, a town twenty miles from the capital, where his grandfather, Emperor Paul I, had himself sought immunity. Here, at Gatchina, everything had a flavor of a garrison, almost a fortress town. The neatness of the streets, the luxuriant greenery of the huge park, the forbidding walls and fences concealed an all-pervading emptiness and lack of life. There was no one to admire the crystal-clear and quiet waters of the Gatchina lakes except the silent swans and equally silent silhouettes of the palace guards who day and night tirelessly walked in and around the park, protecting the Tsar from the menacing eyes of ill-wishers.

Every trip of the Emperor, be it to the capital, or anywhere else in Russia, involved a series of complex protective measures. Never did the people know the time schedule of the imperial train. Endless files of sentinels stood on both sides of the track along the whole length of the route—they stood with their backs turned to the passing train and allowed no one within shouting distance.

Once, under everybody's eyes, a peasant floating downstream on a raft was shot to death by a guard. He had not been able to stop his raft in time and had drifted under the bridge just as the royal train was passing by.

Painstaking measures were also taken to frustrate any attempt at poisoning the monarch. Provisions for the royal table were bought daily, always in different places, and the dealers never knew for whom the purchases were made. A vast number of cooks and assistants were on call every day, but the same persons never serviced the kitchens two days in succession. The names of those who were to be on duty at any particular time were announced at the last moment and always unexpectedly. At the table, surrounded by his family and closest friends, Alexander III would not touch the food until all others had partaken of the fare with no visible ill-effects.

**

All these extraordinary security measures, however, proved insufficient. Plots against the life of Tsar Alexander III were worked out and put into execution. One such plot was to be carried out on March 1, 1887. The terrorists had planned a repetition of "March 1st."

This time the police was able to uncover the machination and a few minutes before the Emperor's passage the terrorists were apprehended on the main street at Gatchina. On their persons were found the bombs they were to hurl at the monarch. Leader of the conspirators was Alexander Ulianov (elder brother of Vladimir Ulianov-Lenin) a name up to then unknown to history. He did not deny his intention, nor did any of the other accomplices attempt to clear their names. Those were fanatics of the revolutionary movement: they did not repent and even refused to petition for leniency. Only the leader's mother, Maria Ulianova, addressed the Emperor with a heartfelt petition in which she beseeched the Tsar, father of the people, not to destroy her mother's heart and to give her son Alexander back to her embrace. She, the mother, gave an oath that with the power of her motherly love she would be able to direct her son onto a righteous path, re-educating him into a good citizen.

Alexander III made the following notation on her appeal: "Fool, what were you thinking about before?" At the same time he sent her Ulianov's confession and ordered mother and son to meet at the prison—"So that she may understand what kind an individual he is." The meeting took place and after that Maria Ulianova did not renew her plea to the Tsar. Leniency was shown towards some of the culprits, but the leaders, Alexander Ulianov among them, were hanged on May 6, 1887, according to sentence by the Military Court.

Did Tsar Alexander III insure the safety of his dynasty by means of this execution? And if so, for how long? Did he know that Maria Ulianova had another son, Vladimir? Did it cross the Tsar's mind what a role history was preparing for the latter and that he would soon be known under the ominous name of Vladimir Ulianov-Lenin, originator and leader of bolshevism? But history loves, it needs contrasts. Thirty years separate that day of execution from another day when that same younger brother of the executed men, by now having become the all-powerful chairman of the Moscow Soviet People's Commissariat, in turn issued a sentence of death. In accordance with that sentence the whole Imperial family was shot in the city of Ekaterinburg, in the cellar of the house belonging to the merchant, Ipatiev. Under the executioners' bullets fell Tsar Nicholas II, the Tsarina, the heir to the throne and four princesses.

But at the time of the hanging of Alexander Ulianov this somber event was still far in the future.

Still another plot against Alexander III's life was organized and this time carried out, even though unsuccessfully, by a group of terrorists who remained unidentified. The date was April 1888 and the occasion a trip of the Tsar and his family through the Kharkov province.

The conspirators managed, in spite of all precautionary measures, to disjoin a section of track near the station of Borki. As a result, in the deep of night, the royal train was derailed, the locomotive and cars rolled down the embankment aid were smashed with great loss of lives and many injuries. Miraculously, due to an incredible combination of circumstances, Alexander III and his family remained unharmed.

This frightful calamity and immediate deadly danger, involving the very person of the Tsar, doubtlessly made a huge impression on Alexander III. But he did not show any sign of fear or confusion and personally on the spot directed rescue operations. Later, a chapel and a magnificent temple named after Christ the Saviour were erected on the spot in memory of the miraculous escape from danger by the Imperial family.

One wonders whether this near-catastrophe did not still further strengthen in the mind of Alexander III the conviction of the right of his reactionary political courses and of the necessity to continue the merciless struggle against all kinds and forms of subversion.

***

Was Alexander III really a despot?

As a guardian of autocracy, Emperor Alexander III did not have any personal instinctive inclination to despotism. He did not have any personal vanity. He was a dedicated man, dedicated with all his being to Russia. He served it as he knew best and, serving, gave it all his strength.

He wore himself out with hard work, spending long nocturnal hours in his study where not even his wife was permitted to enter. Alexander was first of all a man of routine, a conservative in the full meaning of this word. He did not like to change ministers. Throughout his reign he kept the Minister for Foreign Affairs—Girs, and the same War Minister—Vanovski. Alas, these were not the enlightened collaborators of Alexander II. The Tsar had long cleared his cabinet and his court of their presence.

Alexander III never broke the laws which he instituted. It may be that had he inherited a constitutional crown, he would not have done violence to the Constitution nor to the rights of Parliament. The Tsar's character was direct. Thanks to this, court life during his reign was freed of intrigue and favoritism. It is true that there came to exist around him a group of so-called "close" people, such as General Cherevin, Count Vorontsov-Dashkov, and others. But these figures had no political influence at court.

The Emperor relied on his cabinet alone in dealing with affairs of state. In choosing his collaborators he was never guided by intrigue or family tradition. Pobedonostsev came from the clergy, while the celebrated minister of finance Witte began his career as master of a small railroad station.

Having once chosen a person for a certain post, Alexander III always gave that individual his complete trust. Woe to him, however, if that trust was ever abused!

ALEXANDER III AND THE HEIR TO THE THRONE

In his family life Alexander III was simple, but strict and harsh. He was not above applying measures of physical correction in the matter of his children's upbringing. The hand of the father was as firm as the hand of the monarch.

His views on family life were remarkably patriarchal. He was a devoted, model husband. Court rumors even had it that he bad never known intercourse with a woman before his marriage to the Danish Princess Dagmar. To the end of his days he remained faithful to his wife. But not even for her would he abandon his principles and he never allowed her to intrude into affairs of state.

Nor did the so-called Grand Dukes, numerous immediate relatives of the Tsar, escape his iron fist. When Grand Duke Mikhailovich was bold enough to marry a woman of non-royal blood, Countess Merenburg, without asking the Tsar permission to do so, Alexander III not only took away his rank and deprived him of all privileges, but expelled him from the country. Such an example produced a tremendous impression on the other Grand Dukes and nothing similar was ever again attempted under Alexander III.

True, in the realm of marriages, the Tsar was not entirely independent and left such matters to the authority of his wife, the Empress Maria (Dagmar). But beyond that subject "a wench understands nothing," as Alexander put it, and the ambitious Empress Maria, whenever she wanted to influence her husband in any way, had to act through Count Vorontsov-Dashkov, devoted to her and best friend of the Tsar.

Alexander III had three sons and two daughters. The oldest was Nicholas, heir to the throne. At first the parents showed little care and tenderness towards that frail little boy with a thin neck and beautiful blue eyes inherited from his mother. Nor did the Emperor favor his second son—George—stricken with an incurable disease, tuberculosis, which led him to an early grave.

The youngest son, Michael, a red-cheeked boy, alert and healthy, was the Tsar's favorite. Nicholas, always deathly afraid of his strict father, could only observe from a distance Mishka's merry pranks. He shuddered at the thought of what would happen to him if only he dared…. But coming from Mishka's lips, the jokes brought forth only the laughter of the Monarch, a laughter that at times shook all his big and portly body.

Here is a scene, taken from life, concerning the activities of the royal family. The adults are sitting on the terrace. Below it, Mishka plays in the sand. In a jolly mood, Alexander III picks up a sprinkling can and, beckoning to Mishka, pours some water over the boy. Laughter, shrill laughter of the child, the Emperor's deep roar, the respectful smiles of those present.

"Go change, Misha. You are all wet and muddy."

But the boy ignores this. "I got sprinkled. Now it's your turn. Go take my place."

And here is Misha, on the terrace, pushing his father. "Go on, papa, quick!"

"What is fair is fair." As he is, in uniform, Alexander III goes down the steps and stands, patiently waiting, while the impish son empties the watering can onto his balding pate.

Satisfied with one another, excited, father and son go off to the palace to change. Timid, frowning, Nicholas has watched this scene. He can't even dream of such unceremonious conduct towards his father.

No one, it seemed, gave a serious thought to the destiny of this boy, to the importance of his future role. Himself a man lacking a solid education, Alexander III devoted most of his energies to the suppression in his country of the revolutionary movement. He did not realize how important it was to give to his heir a thorough and correct education. The early years of the boy's life passed in an atmosphere of solitude, neglect and fright. Even in the infant Nicholas' character one could observe that depression, confusion, boredom, sense of persecution that are so often found in unloved children.

The question arises: are these traits of character the embryonic beginning of the personality that was to be so peculiar to the Tsar Nicholas in future years?

***

As Nicholas became a little older, Alexander III decided to put him in the hands of an English Tutor, a Mr. Heath, a well-educated man in his own way, excellent sportsman and artist.

When this middle-aged, man, with the healthy handsome face of a typical British sportsman, first appeared at the royal dinner table, young Nicholas greeted him coolly. After supper, as an ice-breaker, Mr. Heath suggested a game. But Nicholas, with a pomposity clashing violently with his modest, appealing little figure, drew himself up aid said: "How can I play with you? I am a prince—you are just an old man."

The shrewd Englishman, entirely unaffected, then grabbed

the "prince" and lifting him in his brawny arms, began to tickle him, at the same time telling him a joke about a pedigreed pig who was inordinately proud of the length of its tail. A few minutes later the room was filled with the boy's cheerful, uninhibited laughter.

The influence of this tutor, however, was limited to the sphere of games, sports and foreign languages. Nobody strove to impress upon the heir the importance of his future role.

Nicholas himself realized it but dimly. The program of the prince's formal education was planned well and on a vast scale. Alexander III approved this program, but did nothing to alleviate routine. By his express orders, General Danilov, an obtuse, unimaginative man with no conception of the importance of his tremendous task, was entrusted with the supervision and regulation of the prince's studies. Moreover, he was required to be personally present at all the lessons. This presence greatly hampered the pedagogical activity of the teachers, especially of those with liberal inclinations. The results became very soon apparent. In his own intimate diary Nicholas wrote quite frankly (January 11, 1890) that he often came close to falling asleep during his lessons from boredom and fatigue.

The opinions of the pedagogues concerning the results of such schooling were quite reserved. In their reports they never saw fit to mention any kind of curiosity or eagerness for learning on the part of the future Tsar. Nor was the situation any better in the purely military field. According to the program, the Crown Prince was to acquaint himself with all existing types of service and actually serve not only in the infantry and cavalry, but even in the fleet. This fact immediately threw the Crown Prince into the milieu which, from then on, was to become the most real and vivid influence in the life of the young man—the milieu of officer camaraderie in the Guards regiments where Nicholas served his military apprenticeship.

But there existed still another influence—that of the tight circle of Grand Dukes, uncles and cousins of the Prince. This influence manifested itself mostly in matters pertaining to the "art of living": amusements, night-life, and a long series of unofficial romances and love affairs. Oddly enough, the stern Alexander III considered such a life-school useful for the future Tsar. "Let him sow his wild oats while he is young," he remarked on one occasion. "It will make him calmer later on."

This is the kind of atmosphere in which Nicholas spent the golden years of his youth—years in which any young man, no matter of what station, should strive to reap from school and life the knowledge and experience available.

***

The general pattern of Alexander III's daily life was never characterized by luxury. To the contrary, it was almost shocking in its simplicity and modesty. The Imperial Family did not live in the sumptuous halls of the immense Gatchina palace. Probably for greater security, they lived in the basement, in rooms occupied under Paul I by the servants. "There isn't even enough room for the grand piano," complained the Empress Maria.

"Never mind, never mind. We shall put in an upright," her

august husband promised in consolation.

It was, of course, utterly impossible to cram the mastodonic palace furniture into those rooms. Simple "bourgeois" armchairs and couches pushed against the walls made up the royal decor. The ceilings were so low that one could touch them with one's hands. For the tall, powerful frame of the Emperor all this was obviously inadequate. Yet this very modesty seemed to please Alexander III.

The quarters were so restricted, even in number of rooms, that when the Queen of Greece, Olga, came for a visit, she had to spend her nights in the bathroom connecting the royal bedrooms. Alexander III was especially fond of Queen Olga and wanted her as near to him as possible—but no other accommodation was available!

In his family relationships Alexander III was not only careful, but even parsimonious. Even the photographs which Empress Maria collected with such loving care, had to be fastened to the wall without frames, by means of lowly thumbtacks!

This was the picture of the uncomplicated family life of the Russian Tsar Alexander III. Here in this modest corner of the palace, time flowed not as in a center of power tremendous in its scope, where the destinies of then 150 million souls were forged, but rather as within the limited circle of family and household interests.

INTERNATIONAL AFFAIRS

On the other hand, official receptions and balls during the reign of Alexander III were absolutely exceptional for their pomp. Nothing remotely approaching then in glitter, wealth and pomp could be seen in any other court of Europe. This was entirely a different matter, having nothing to do with the life of the private individual, but a matter pertaining to the state, to the dignity and prerogatives of the autocratic power of the Tsar for which Alexander III had the highest degree of respect and which—it must be admitted—he knew how to preserve.

Whatever Alexander III did, he did it with impeccable outer dignity: whether he governed the state, or worshipped God, or shouted to his troops a rugged "Thank you!", received ambassadors, gave orders to the ministers, or pulled on his boots, or steamed himself in a steam bath. In this dignity there was concealed a great force, not so much of a moral as of a physical order. His powerful build alone produced a great effect on the masses. The people saw in him the image of a true Tsar.

This image, not entirely devoid of artificial traits, bore in itself an imposing, at times even hypnotizing power. Once it even saved the life of the famous Russian surgeon-anatomist Grubbe who, in dissecting a corpse, had contracted an infection that threatened general blood poisoning. An immediate operation was needed to save his life. Such an operation however, could not be performed because of the extremely weak condition of the patient. The situation was indeed desperate. Alexander III, learning of the plight of the Russian scientist, victim of his duty, sent Grubbe a well-wishing personal telegram. The sole idea that he had received a personal message from the all-powerful autocrat of all the Russians so impressed the dying man and gave him such a lift, that the attending physicians decided to take advantage of the opportunity and perform the operation. Thus the life of the scientist was saved.

Alexander III put too much value on the prestige of his power to fall under the influence of any one person. If he did listen, as for instance when Pobedonostsev counseled, it was solely because the views expressed coincided closely to his own. But decisions were taken by Alexander III himself, with the aid of his extraordinary will power. This man was firm, averse to favoritism, honest after his own fashion. But above all he was coarse and simple, as coarse and simple were the people he ruled.

Alexander III was a "peasant on the throne," a title which is a compliment in our democratic age. And it must be said that his sympathies lay with the peasants, even though during his reign nothing substantial was done to better their lot. Still, peasant Russia, freed from slavery during the preceding reign, continued ever under Alexander III to revere in the Tsar a symbolic image of the greatness and glory of Russia, convinced that the Tsar was full of love for the people, that the Tsar would of his own free will give the people all they needed: freedom and land.

***

"When the Russian Tsar is out fishing, Europe can wait," said Alexander III once when his minister for foreign affairs begged him to hurry with a decision on a question of urgent importance for all major European powers. But the Emperor was fishing in the Baltic sea and… Europe waited, straining to hear the voice of the northern colossus.

Such utterances were not bravado, not vain boasting of a dictator. They revealed the calm and sure realization by Alexander III of his power. True, this power was based on millions of people, on obscure and silent masses, but the Tsar believed in the power of these masses and therefore in matters of foreign policy acted with the same conscious sureness which he showed in everything else.

Alexander III put considerable effort and time into a fundamental, multilateral study of the international situation. He mounted the throne at a particularly crucial moment in history: the authority of the Iron Chancellor Bismarck reigned supreme all over Europe. Alexander III, well aware of his own unpreparedness both in experience and education, heeded the cautiousness so deeply in his character and for a long time strove to keep as much as possible away from the international scene. He observed events as they developed and tried to avoid any initiative that could provoke complications. He willingly listened to advice, but… all final decisions were always his own.

"The Russian question is simple," finally announces the Tsar, having by now become familiar with every twist of European politics. "Russia occupies one sixth of the globe!"

Unlike his internal policy, in which his mind was

concentrated on one principle, and one subject only—safe-guarding the principle of absolutism—Alexander III's foreign policy was characterized by all the best qualities of his nature: caution, clarity of thought, firmness and even straightforwardness. He could not abide intrigues, behind the scene play, hypocrisy. He did not hide his mistrust of the German Emperor Wilhelm II and of the Iron Chancellor, Prince Bismarck. In answer to a flattering speech by the Kaiser concerning the allegedly existing friendship between the two Emperors, Alexander III, well aware of the behind the scene machinations carried on by Germany against Russia, answered at a dinner in Gatchina with the following thundering toast: "I drink to the health of my only friend, the King of Montenegro!"

Giving special attention to matters of foreign affairs and being, in fact, the sole leader in such matters, Alexander III desired the whole world to know that the Tsar himself and no one else directed the foreign policies of the Russian Empire. His point of view was well founded. Such an awareness helped raise the prestige of Russia in the world. As proof of this we have the fact that, in spite of the friendship ties between the dynasties of Hohenzollern and Hapsburgs the young Emperor Wilhelm II, upon ascending the throne, made haste to choose the Russian capital for his first state visit, instead of Vienna.

It must be said that his wise Chancellor, Bismarck, did not advise the young Kaiser to go to St. Petersburg, pointing out that Emperor Alexander III was not very fond of being "disturbed in his own house." No one can deny in Bismarck an extraordinary capacity to understand people. He understood perfectly well that the difference in characters between the two rulers was too vast and that a personal meeting between them would in no way help Russo-German relations. On the other hand, perhaps, the Iron Chancellor had other, personal, motives n this matter. It has been said by many that he did not want his young Emperor to gain too much control in the matters of Germany's foreign affairs.

Here is a characteristic detail of the first meeting between the two Emperors. When the fleet bearing the Kaiser approached Kronstadt (a fortified island near St. Petersburg) Alexander III was on the bridge of his yacht "Alexandria" in the company of his brother, Grand Duke Alexis, and of Admiral N. Lomen. Noticing that the fleet had stopped, Alexander III asked the Grand Duke: "Alexis, why are they stuck?"

"They are awaiting the visit of your Majesty," unerringly answered Grand Duke Alexis who was well acquainted with all the rules of ceremonial meetings between crowned heads.

"They will have to wait a long time," snapped the Tsar. "Go, Alexis, fetch the guests and bring them here."

The order of the Tsar was carried out to the letter.

Alexander III took his time with the return visit. More than a year passed before he decided to visit Berlin. Bismarck's pride was deeply offended by such conduct and in retaliation he forbade quoting Russian stock on the Berlin exchange and using it as security against loans. But he issued this order only when he knew that Alexander III was already on his way to Berlin and the royal train could not be stopped without serious diplomatic complications. This circumstance could not fail to touch Alexander III to the quick at the moment of his arrival in Berlin, in spite of the exceptionally grandiose welcome ceremony that awaited him at the station.

Emperor Wilhelm II, the Iron Chancellor, representatives of German states, military and diplomatic hierarchies were present. "At last!" With this exclamation the German official press welcomed the arrival of the Tsar in Berlin on October 11, 1889. While still at the station, Bismarck asked the Russian Tsar for an audience. The meeting took place an hour later in the building of the Russian embassy where, having turned down the accommodations prepared for him in the Kaiser's palace, Alexander III spent his days in Berlin. And here, at this historic meeting, Prince Bismarck's brilliant diplomatic talents were shown in all their magnificence. What happened during that hour is known to the Russian Tsar and the German Chancellor alone. But history is well aware of the fact that the beginning of the audience was stormy. Alexander III did not hide his feelings of mistrust for Germany's general policies, nor did he hide his dissatisfaction at German intrigues in the Balkans, clearly directed against Russia.

Bismarck's convincing rejoinders soothed the Tsar. An hour elapsed and Alexander III gradually gave in to the spell of the Iron Chancellor's personality. Nevertheless, as Count P. Shuvalov later related, a memento of this audience remained in the Berlin embassy: it was a silver ash tray which Alexander III kneaded in his powerful hands during his talk with Bismarck, finally reducing it to a wad of twisted metal.

A glittering reception with the participation of all the diplomatic corps and the highest German society, was given on that same evening in the Kaiser's palace in honor of the Russian Emperor. This was organized according to all the rules of ceremonial etiquette appropriate to such an occasion. All went well, if we forget the name of the fifth course at the dinner: "Chicken à la Metz," a name that could doubtlessly annoy the French and their sympathizers present at the affair. (Metz was the capital and fortress of Lorraine where in the Franco-Prussian war of 1871 the French General Basaine was forced to surrender to the Germans with all his army.)

Alexander III behaved distantly at the banquet and appeared bored. He exchanged a few brief remarks with the people surrounding him and in answer to a lengthy political speech by Wilhelm II, answered with a brief toast, "To the health of the German Emperor Wilhelm II," which he made in a loud, firm voice and in French even though he knew the German language to perfection. After supper the conversation between the two monarchs lagged sorely and the Kaiser ended up talking with the Russian ambassador Count Shuvalov, while Alexander III conferred with Prince Bismarck.

Later, already in retirement, Bismarck was very fond of recalling this conversation with the Russian Tsar. Alexander III made him sit down and talked to him at length, leaning against his chair. In this attention Bismarck chose to see a sign of the trust he thought he had engendered in the Tsar. But it is doubtful that the Tsar's attitude was really a sign of any marked trust. It seems more probable that the Tsar simply wished to have a closer look at such an outstanding political figure of Europe.

Taking leave of Bismarck at the railroad station, Alexander

III addressed him as follows: "Good-bye, Prince. You have convinced me of many things, but can you guarantee that should you leave your post, the Berlin cabinet will not change its policy?"

"Your Majesty," answered Bismarck haughtily, "You may rest assured that I shall die at my post."

Emperor Alexander III was still on his way home when Bismarck began to ponder and to understand the deep meaning of the question thrown at him by the Russian Tsar. The latter knew that the days of the Iron Chancellor as a political figure were already numbered. The favor of the German Kaiser was swiftly shifting elsewhere.

***

Alexander III's purely practical, purely materialistic common sense, unburdened by any theoretical knowledge, permitted him in moments of international stress to be even more penetrating than his well-educated collaborators.

This fact became apparent in the course of one Anglo-Russian conflict. The south-eastern border of Russia touched Afghanistan, a country then under the protectorate of England. On that occasion an Afghan detachment crossed the border and entered deeply into Russian territory. The commander of the Russian border troops, Colonel Komarov, routed the intruders and became so engrossed in the chase that he in turn crossed the river Kushka, which constituted the border, and occupying the region of the Punjab, captured the raiders on foreign territory.

London went up in arms. The press and the minister for

foreign affairs, Marquis of Salisbury, the latter in a note to the Russian Government, insisted on the immediate recall of Colonel Komarov and requested reparations to England from Tsarist Russia. Complications began to arise. Rumors began to fly concerning certain movements of the English fleet and the air was thick with mentions of war. The Russian Minister for Foreign Affairs, Girs, lost his head. The motto of this statesman of the old school was in essence, "Let there be no scandals in my lovely castle." He attempted to insist that Alexander III give full satisfaction to England, whose prestige at the time was at its peak.

In answer to all the confusion created by the incident, Alexander III issued the order that Colonel Komarov be promoted to major-general and decorated into the bargain. Such a bold gesture produced the desired effect in London and the incident closed with a victory of Russian diplomacy.

A similarly original decisiveness, unusual in the ethics of diplomacy, was shown once by Alexander III in connection with the recall by France of its ambassador to the Russian court, General Ampare, for whom the Tsar had a personal feeling of friendship. Alexander III declared that henceforth he refused to have any French ambassador at his court at all. In vain did the French government offer to send one of its most famous generals as a substitute for Ampare. It took much persuasion and a long time to change the mind of the stubborn monarch and make him accept a different ambassador.

But there came a time when international relations changed brusquely with the official refusal by the young Kaiser Wilhelm II to renew the secret military agreement existing between Germany and Russia, thus bringing to an end the traditional ties between the two countries. Bismarck, the German Iron Chancellor, went into complete retirement. On the eve of this step Bismarck summoned the Russian Ambassador Count Shuvalov to inform him of the impending event and to tell him that one of the principal causes thereof was Wilhelm's accusation that Bismarck had become excessively Russophile.

The new international political situation alarmed the Russian ministry for foreign affairs. In fact, the traditional Russo-German friendship had long been an important factor and guarantee of a lasting peace in Europe. Now there arose the obvious necessity for a closer rapprochement with France. Alexander III winced at the step, but gradually renouncing all his former prejudices against the French republican system, finally decided to make a treaty of friendship with France. This was to be a step of the utmost importance, shifting as it did the whole balance of power and political equilibrium in Europe.

In order to invest the event with even greater significance the French government sent a fleet into Russian waters. A special ceremony was organized on one of the French warships, with the scheduled participation of Tsar Alexander III himself. But suddenly there came a moment of wild apprehension— what should be done with the French national anthem, the Marseillaise? The absolute ruler of all Russias and a revolutionary anthem! Alexander III, hearing of this, allays all fears with the remark: "I am not a sufficiently good musician to compose a new anthem for the French." And when the moment came he listened with his customary self-control to the Marseillaise, that composition by Rouget de L'Isle the sounds of which heretofore he could not tolerate.

Finally, on December 31, 1891 by imperial order, N. Girs, Russian Minister for Foreign Affairs and the Marquis de Montebello, French plenipotentiary, met to sign the first Franco-Russian written agreement. This was to be the beginning of the celebrated Franco-Russian alliance which for a third of a century was to regulate the whole international balance in Europe.

Pathetic in itself was the moment of signing. The Russian Minister Girs, pen in hand, crosses himself and fails silent for a minute. Noticing the astonished look on the face of the French Marquis, he explained: "I have just asked God to stop my hand if in spite of all that my reason tells me, this alliance must spell the end of Russia!" But impartial destiny, that same "Finger of God" which, according to the formula of the Tsarist reactionaries was supposed to lead Imperial Russia along the "path of righteousness," destiny did not stop the hand of the Tsar's minister at that crucial historic moment. Preserving its indifference towards humans, destiny left it up to inflexible truth to untangle by itself the consequences of what had been wrought.

Meanwhile, World War I and its terrifying result for Russia—bloodshed, revolution and the fall of a dynasty—were concealed at the end of that very road that was open for Russia by the document signed on that day.

ILLNESS OF ALEXANDER III

Alexander III's heroic physical build is not to give him longevity.

The Tsar is ill, he suffers from a constant ache in his side. But he bears it in silence. He does not change the order of his life, nor the tempo of his work. He even continues to ride on horseback, attends hunts and revues. Unwilling to lose even a particle of his regal dignity, Alexander III refuses to recognize the authority of medicine and of physicians. He despises them both. For this he is fated to pay a dear price.

His wife at long last is able to convince him that a medical examination is long overdue. Professor Zakhariin of Moscow and, later, Professor Leyden, especially called in from Berlin, diagnose the illness as nephritis, a kidney ailment, in its most serious, threatening form. Their order: immediate move to the south, complete rest and… not a drop of vodka.

Nobody among the Tsar's entourage, not even his wife, have the courage to tell Alexander III about his condition. This task falls on Professor Zakhariin, well known for his authoritative independence and directness. What does Alexander feel, what does he think upon hearing a merciless death sentence from the lips of one of his subjects? The fact that the subject is also a celebrated physician helps not a bit. Alexander will let no one forget that he is first of all a Tsar and will never become the patient of a subject.

He listens to Zakhariin's conclusions with an ironic smile and that same evening, stubbornly, orders a military review, maneuvers near the German border and a hunting party in the

Bielovezhskaia reservation where, quite appropriately a new summer palace is ready, awaiting a personal inspection by the Monarch.

And here is the Tsar in his element on horseback, among his beloved troops, among the game wardens, among the buffaloes felled by his own outstanding marksmanship. He delights at the sumptuous picnics in the woods… laced with ice-cold vodka filling the ample royal cup. The Tsar feels in top form, the pain is gone, color is coming back to his cheeks. Alexander considers himself recovered. But this state of euphoria comes to a sudden end—a seizure, vomiting, swelling of the feet and ankles…. The Tsar is put to bed and urgently transported to Crimea, to the warm shores of the Black Sea.

It seems that the doctors suggested an even warmer climatic station for the august invalid—the island of Corfu in the Ionic Archipelago. This however would involve leaving Russia and never, under any circumstances would the Tsar be willing to take such a step. The doctors are told not even to mention the word Corfu.

The Black Sea fleet, on parade before the shores of Crimea, salutes its Emperor, whose days have already been reckoned. Does the Tsar himself know that he is sentenced to imminent death? Perhaps. But in dying he builds no illusions for himself, just as he never did during his entire life. Death is inevitable: this means it must be accepted. It also means that he must die in the traditional style of regal majesty. Fewer doctors, fewer medicines. Let them summon Father John of Kronstadt. Let them order Te Deums for the Emperor's health all over the country. Regularly, every day, the Tsar follows Father John's advice and holds against his ailing side a miraculous poultice, dark brown, the color of that very earth in which soon he is destined to lie. Suddenly, to everybody's amazement, he orders a woman of the people to be his cook. He is tired of the refinement of palace fare, he says now that he never liked it. And now, in the last days of his life, he nourishes himself with food prepared by a simple peasant woman who, it may be, still remembers the days of her slavery.

The doctors have forbidden Alexander III to get up from bed. In spite of that, Professor Zakhariin once found the Emperor sitting on a chair. In answer to Zakhariin's question as to who of the doctors had permitted him to do so, Alexander III says: "I am doing it with the permission of the Emperor of Russia." It is rumored in court circles that Professor Zakhariin, in view of the frequent infractions by the Tsar of his medical orders, wants to leave the Livadia Palace. But the palace Commandant, General Cherevin, threatens to hold him by force if necessary at the bedside of the imperial patient.

In spite of pain, in spite of physical incapacity, Alexander III continues to conduct all affairs of state, personally signing all important papers that are sent to him from the capital by special courier. With superhuman efforts, with the stubbornness of a maniac, at times falling asleep over his work, he continues at the helm of the state. He even refuses to put on a comfortable robe, but continues to wear his general's uniform and never utters a word of complaint in the presence of outsiders. And all this in order not to lose even a particle of his regal dignity. For hours he sits on the balcony of the palace, listening to the army band as it plays his favorite marches and to the marvelous harmonies of the Cossack choir. This is the only relaxation for the Tsar in the last hours of his life.

And then, suddenly, one more order. The heir to the throne must marry without delay! But who is to be the bride? The Princess Alice of Hessen? Nicholas has long been in love with Alice of Hessen and in the innermost sanctum of his heart he indeed hopes that, someday she will become his wife.

PRINCESS ALICE OF HESSEN

The Princess Alice of Hessen was an orphan. She was only six at the death of her mother, the Grand Duchess of Hessen Darmstadt, daughter of England's Queen Victoria. Ever since she had lived at the British court, under Victoria's tutelage. Victoria loved her granddaughter and took her along wherever she went—to Windsor, Balmoral and Sandringham. At court, Alice is brought up on par with her British royal cousins. She is taught languages, history and other subjects, she is dressed like her cousins and gets the same pleasures as they do, she attends sports events, theatres, balls, she receives all the signs of respect due to a member of a royal house.

One would think that in her life at the British court nothing could occur to wound the pride of an adolescent. But Alice in no way resembled other, balanced young girls.

One must delve deeply into the recesses of this complex, enigmatic soul with all its psychic and moral twists in order to understand the twilight epoch of Russian Tsarism, at the center of which stood Alice, the future Tsarina Alexandra. Tall, straight, with a handsome, rather stiff face, with a character that would not allow her to bend, Princess Alice was an introvert, proud, passionate, imperious. Her nature did not fit at all into any common mold. No trait of her character alone can be understood without the context of her soul's many peculiarities. It seemed that there were in her more masculine than feminine traits.

"Oh, if only I were a man!" was her favorite exclamation. But there was in her one trait, specifically feminine, which changed and disrupted all the other elements. This trait was hysteria, a trait which she had inherited from her mother together with a tendency towards mysticism tinted with religious superstition. Under pressure from this trait the reason part of her character had given in to the emotional. Who knows, perhaps it was in this very lack of stability, in the very nucleus of this spiritual anomaly that was hidden the strength of the future Tsarina Alexandra of Russia.

With her personality it was not easy for Alice to resign herself to a position of foster child, even in the bosom of a royal family. Dry, dutiful rather than spontaneous are her responses to the salutes of the fur-hatted guards at Buckingham Palace, for such signs of honor do not speak to her pride. She seems to think that it is not to her personally that these honors are directed. And her feeling is the same as she listens to the greetings of the crowds during her outings with the royal family. It is amazing how many alarming doubts crowded her young soul! She constantly kept seeing nuances of some imagined nonexisting unequality. And yet, at the same time, in her secretive, precocious mind, she is perfectly able to analyze and evaluate the content of the outwardly brilliant royal atmosphere which surrounds her. And it appears to her as not imposing enough, simply as the sumptuous outer shell of a power which has already lost its actual strength. This outer shell seems to Alice quite different from what true royal power should be, the kind of power about which she has already copiously read in the beautifully bound volumes of history in her grandmother's library. How far all this was in Alice's eyes from that limitless grandeur of near divine Tsarist power about which she had heard so much from her older sister Elizabeth married to the Russian Grand Duke Serge, brother of Tsar Alexander III.

But there did come a day when finally Princess Alice found herself in the Russian capital, a guest of her sister. "Here is St. Petersburg. And this is Russia." And there she is in the kingdom of snows, churches and Orthodox liturgical singing, a gilded and flattering court retinue and 150 million of kind, bearded, loyal peasants.... She finds herself at the Winter Palace, at a splendid court ball. The storybook luxury and wealth of the Russian Imperial Court immediately captivates, charms and overwhelms the passionate nature of the Princess.

With a feeling of trembling adoration Alice gazes at the heroic figure of Alexander III, unlimited master of the Russian Empire in whose hands, she knows well, there is a power unequaled anywhere in the world. At the ball, in the huge room with malachite columns, lit by numberless candles, she is introduced to a nice-looking, blue-eyed youth in a tight military uniform. He begins to court her so sweetly. He dances with her. He brings her orangeade and candy.... And as a farewell he kisses her hand and murmurs: "I shall never forget you."

This blue-eyed youth is Nicholas, the heir of the Russian throne.

But time goes on. Princess Alice is invited to Peterhof where the Imperial Family spends the summer. She lives with them, sees the ruler and his retinue in more intimate surroundings. And she herself is observed, appraised, ceaselessly watched until the day arrives for her to return to England.

And what was the result of all the testing? The strict court etiquette forbade to mention it aloud. Voices remained silent. But Princess Alice was able to notice something even more explicit than words during her stay in Peterhof and especially during her last evening there. This something, so eloquent, was the marble-cold expression of the face of the Empress mother, with its frozen smile. It was also the confused, embarrassed face of the Heir. And it was the crowd of courtiers—only recently they had fawned over her, now they were too obviously reserved. On that evening the court music roared in Alice's ears like thunder in a nightmare, the famous Peterhof fountains and the bronze statues shone reflecting the lights and seemed to underscore her humiliation.

But there was a man in that brilliant court multitude who astonished Alice. He did not diminish, but rather doubled his respectful attention towards her, he seemed anxious to smooth away the offensive tactlessness of the others. There was something chivalrous shining in his handsome, distinguished face when he greeted her in the park, served her a drink, and on the last day appeared at the station and followed the train with a sad and soulful gaze. This handsome officer was Prince Orloff. Alice remembered him and later she knew how to reward him. But for that she had to become the Empress of Russia.

How could this brief encounter smooth away the tormenting sense of insult thrown at the proud Princess by the Russian Court? Alice however had a puritan self-control, she had will power. Upon returning to England she revealed none of her heartbreak and we cannot know at the price of what tormenting efforts, of what bitter tears she was able to achieve her show of indifference.

It was a failure which she had felt deeply, but which still somehow seemed inconceivable. It became completely obvious however, when Alice reached the age of nineteen. Queen Victoria, anxious to arrange a marriage between her granddaughter and the heir to the Russian throne, anxious at the delay, decided to "Take matters into her own hands." Taking advantage of her status as Queen, she wrote directly to the Russian Empress. She described how Alice, after her St. Petersburg visit, had become interested in everything Russian, how she had fallen in love with Russia. Further on, "casually," she asked whether any of the members of the Imperial Family had especially liked Alice. She, the Queen, was interested in knowing this in order to be guided in the further education of the Princess.

Queen Victoria probably thought this a subtle, clever letter. She received a no less sly answer in the following terms: The interest shown by Princess Alice for everything Russian deeply pleased the Tsar and Tsarina. The further direction of the Princess' education however should depend exclusively on the taste of the young girl herself and on the wish of the crowned guardian. As for any romantic involvement on the part of any member of the Royal Family, the Tsarina was aware of nothing of the sort. Even had there been some such sort of childish feelings, she was certain that they were by now long forgotten.

What a cruel, undeserved blow to the pride of the poor Princess!

But what about Nicholas himself? What was he feeling? What were his thoughts about Princess Alice? Here is an entry into his intimate diary of that time: "My dream is someday to marry Alice of Hessen. I have loved her for a long time. For a long time I have resisted this feeling, trying to fool myself by the impossibility of ever bringing alive this secret dream of mine." And Nicholas really loved her, loved her deeply, seriously. But he could not find within himself enough strength to fight for his feeling. He was absolutely incapable of standing up for it. He was timid, modest, passive. He was deathly afraid of his harsh father, couldn't even admit the thought of ever contradicting him in this matter and could not even find enough decisiveness within himself to contradict his own mother.

Once when the Empress Maria mentioned marriage and cited somebody else's name, Nicholas listened in silence, without protest, and later noted in the diary: "I want to go in one direction, but my mother wants me to follow another."

"What is going to happen?" he noted later in that same

diary, seemingly uncertain as to what such conditions could wreak with the feeling so intensely dominating his soul. What is going to happen? That was going to happen which was even then being dispassionately prepared for Imperial Russia by a pitiless destiny and which nobody, neither Alexander III, nor Nicholas, nor Princess Alice could possibly foresee.

The moment was near. The death of Alexander III imminent. People close to the throne were worried, were even beginning to lose their heads. In the crisis, confronted by the unavoidable, Empress Maria was somehow able to overcome her own aversion towards the suggested bride and personally convinced Alexander III to give his approval for the match.

Did not on that day Imperial Russia make another fatal leap, another giant step towards its own destruction?

Meanwhile, on the southern shores of Russia, the sunny clear days preceding the death of Alexander III, became for Nicholas days of personal happiness. His fiancée to be, Alice, was at that time staying with the Duchess of Coburg and arrangements were immediately made for Nicholas' departure for Germany. Emperor Wilhelm II, who was extremely interested in a marriage between the Heir to the Russian throne and a German Princess, also hurried to Coburg.

Upon his arrival to Coburg, the shy Nicholas characteristically demurred with his proposal and it took the energetic intervention of Wilhelm himself, prompted by his own calculations, to precipitate the event. Finally on April 8, 1894, Nicholas of Russia and Alice of Hessen became engaged. The German Emperor was so pleased that on the next day, meeting the British military attaché in the street, he exclaimed:

"You may congratulate me! Nicky is engaged and it cost me no little effort. I had to pour almost a whole bottle of champagne into him to give him courage."

Nicholas, on his part, in his diary, calls this day "the most wonderful, unforgettable day of my life." And he adds: "At this moment I would so terribly like to glance into the depth of Alice's soul."

Next, the engaged couple spent some time together in London at the British Court. They took boat rides on the Thames, rowing together. Alice filled the still empty pages of his diary with tender words and quotes from her favorite poems and songs. The month spent in England was to be one of the most pleasant and luminous periods in Nicholas' life.

On one occasion in Windsor palace the Prince of Wales, the future King Edward VII, jokingly asked Princess Alice what sort of a wife was she planning to make for her betrothed. She answered: "Faithful, loving, dedicated and strong as death." These were not empty words. They reflected precisely every wrinkle in the soul of the future Russian Empress Alexandra. On Princess Alice's lips they sounded like an oath, a program for a future life—a program which she was to carry out with terrifying precision.

Meanwhile Nicholas had to hurry back to Livadia, to the deathbed of his father. And here, in Livadia, he awaited with impatience the arrival of his beloved fiancée. Bell-ringing, delegations, flowers met the woman who even recently had been considered an unwelcome guest in this country and whom many evil court tongues had nicknamed "The Hessen Fly." Alexander III, in spite of his illness, put on his general's parade uniform and the high boots that could hardly be pulled onto his swollen legs. In spite of doctors' orders he got up from bed and, solemnly, as behooves an autocrat, came out to meet the future Russian Empress.

Alice's first gesture upon arriving to Russia was characteristic. She expressed the desire to take on the Russian Orthodox faith. When this was done, she became the betrothed of the Heir according to the rites of the Church. This was in no way a betrothal dictated by political calculation, as so often happens between members of various reigning families. This was a betrothal brought about by love in the full sense of the word. On May 6 of that same year, on his twenty-sixth birthday, Nicholas wrote: "I am nearer to 30 than to 20…. But on the other hand I am engaged. And to whom? To such a treasure, to such a divine creature as Alice…."

But after that divine fiancée had lived at Livadia for a certain time, the court circles began feeling the imperious hand of the future Tsarina Alexandra. Allowed by Nicholas to read his diary, the adored fiancée made an entry into it herself, dated October 15, in which she tried to convince Nicholas to insist that the course of his father's illness be reported to him before it reached anybody else. "Do not let anybody forget who you are," was the advice of the sharp fiancée to her betrothed.

Her observant eyes had already clearly seen out of what human material she would have to mold the future autocrat. Even at that early date she was already attempting to straighten out his short physical build, improve his posture, strengthen his voice. Like an experienced director she was already rehearsing him in the role of limitlessly powerful monarch.

DEATH OF ALEXANDER III

Alexander III was living out his last days. Neither the doctors, nor the climate could be of any help. His strength ebbed visibly with every passing hour. His eyes receded deeper and deeper into their orbits and the shadows of death lay ever heavier on his emaciated cheeks. The last days of his life were burdened with heavy misgivings. Above all he was tormentingly worried about the future. Thoughts about the fate of his autocratic rule, to which he had given all his strength and ability, gnawed at him night and day.

Could the dying Tsar believe that his son Nicholas would be able to cope with the task of governing a state? It is doubtful. Alexander III better than anybody else knew what an iron hand was required for a successful functioning by the autocratic state machine. Had not he himself tightened its every bolt and joint with such a hand? On the other hand, when Nicholas, the Heir to the throne, foreseeing the thorny future and frightened by all the talk about it, attempted to hint at his desire to abdicate his rights, Alexander III exploded into an uncontrolled rage. He could not tolerate any deviation from the laws of succession. He was determined to enforce their inviolability. From his deathbed he dictates and forces his son to sign in advance the manifesto proclaiming the accession to the throne of Nicholas II, Emperor of all Russias.

On October 19 the Tsar glanced for the last time out of his window in the Livadia palace. One could see from his eyes that he was happy to die within the boundaries of his own fatherland. October 20 was to be the day of Alexander III's passing. His breath was labored, his heavy body shocked by convulsions. Pale and lost, members of his family crowded the ample divan on which he lay dying. Each one of them had long become accustomed to the thought of an inevitable end, but now that the moment is actually at hand they were mute and afraid.

Father John of Kronstadt alone was not perturbed. Kneeling by the bedside he held up the dying man's head with one hand and pressed something against his lips with the other. That was the Chalice with the Holy Sacraments. Father John performed his function calmly, as if the divine mystery had truly been revealed to him and he could by his actions insure his Emperor of eternal rest and immortality in the Kingdom of the One to whom alone Alexander had been willing to bow and in the Name of whom he had ruled the peoples of Russia.

It was exactly 2:15 in the afternoon when Emperor Alexander III exhaled his last breath. At 4:00 p.m. the palace Chaplain, Father Ianyshev, made preparations for ceremonial function pertaining to life rather than death—receiving the oath of allegiance from the Imperial Family, the Court and the palace garrison in the name of the new Monarch.

Father Ianyshev had not yet had time to recover from the acute sense of hurt and insult which he had felt that very morning when he had been unable to wrest from John of Kronstadt the right to attend the Emperor's passing into a better world. He had felt this to be his right as Chaplain of the Court and the intervention of the astute intruder had opened a wound which was to fester in his heart the rest of his life.

But an unexpected event, unforeseen by the rules, occurred at that point and Father Ianyshev was forced to put off the oath ceremony. The Empress Maria refused to give allegiance to her own son Nicholas, in spite of the categorical requisites of the law of succession.

"Russia will perish under his rule," she declared simply and frankly.

The courtiers and ministers present at Livadia completely lost their heads before the emergency that threatened to get out of hand. Many already foresaw the possibility of changes in the laws of succession, others expected a palace coup. The brother of the deceased Emperor, Grand Duke Vladimir, anxiously awaiting news in St. Petersburg, was especially interested in the latter eventuality. Excitement and confusion grew by the hour, but no one had the temerity to approach the Empress and demand that she comply with the law.

Finally the Governor of Odessa, Count Musin-Pushkin was summoned as a man celebrated for his decisiveness and presence of mind. Followed by a crowd of courtiers the latter marched "straight against the enemy." Entering the chambers of the Empress he solemnly proclaimed Nicholas II Emperor of all the Russias. His voice was loud and permitted no rebuttal. The courtiers, encouraged by his leadership, immediately supported him with loud hurrahs. The Empress' partisans, headed by Count Vorontsov-Dashkov, were unprepared and not influential enough to come to her aid and she had no course left to her but to bow before an accomplished fact.

This incident remained a secret of the Russian Imperial

Court. It did not leak out into the press nor to the people and was even kept from high society. In fact, information concerning all that happened at Livadia both before and after Alexander III's death was extremely scarce, meted out in the form of brief official communiqués or bulletins. Apparently the palace censorship was unwilling to undermine the authority of autocratic power by useless news of internal strife.

Even the Emperor's passing was not announced at once. As anatomists-surgeons Vilkovski and Vyvodtsev were leaving the capital for Livadia to embalm the body of the Tsar, the St. Petersburg Metropolitan, in the presence of anxious throngs of people at the St. Isaac Cathedral, said a solemn mass "for the recovery of Alexander III." The Russian diplomatic representatives abroad were informed of the Tsar's demise with great delay. Because of this fact, some of them found themselves in a very delicate position. Thus, for instance, in Berlin the German press announced the death of the Russian Tsar as early as 4 o'clock that afternoon and at 7 o'clock all the royal theatres officially cancelled their performances in sign of mourning. At 8:00 p.m., the Russian Ambassador, Count Shuvalov, having received no confirmation from his government, considered it his duty to present a formal protest against an unjustified mourning. One hour later, however, having finally received the news from Livadia, he was forced to retract his protest and to apologize for his lack of information.

Meanwhile in Livadia the palace authorities were already engaged in the organization of an extraordinary ceremonial program concerning the return of the Tsar's body to the capital. For the first time since the death of Alexander I the body of a Tsar was to travel across all of Russia to be interred in the capital, resting place of Russian Emperors. The process of the funeral itself was thereby considerably lengthened and much was added to the disruption of all affairs of state usual in such contingencies. But on the other hand the whole ceremony could assume a character of exceptional solemnity and the expression of popular grief could be played upon on a much vaster scale.

According to tradition the funeral could not be hastened in any unseemly way. Even the coffin could not be sealed, nor even closed. Everybody had to see the Tsar's body, see it in its traditional grandeur. Moscow, Petersburg, the Guards, the Court, the ministers, foreign ambassadors and delegations, the Russian people—all those who had known this man strong, healthy and all-powerful were now to see him dead, but still magnificent and dignified.

Such was the program. But the Tsar's body, large and heavy, began to decompose with frightful rapidity. The specialists summoned from the capital had to perform miracles of artistry to save the Imperial remains from total destruction and to restore it through embalming to the aspect of greatness required by tradition. At the same time the physicians compiled the protocol concerning the autopsy, a document which the law required be kept in the government archives.

The gunboat "Zaporozhets," immediately dispatched from the capital, brings to Crimea its sad cargo, accompanied by a special guard—several cases, one of them containing the golden Imperial crown and the deceased Monarch's battle sabre which are to be placed on the lid of the coffin. Throngs of people, awed and silent, watch the unloading. Especially impressive are two enormous crates covered with black oil cloth. They contain the two coffins, one of oak and the other of metal. For some reason the solemn transference of the body from the palace to the small local church of the Transfiguration is effected at night, in the flickering light of torches. Here the body will rest until its departure for the capital. The doors of the church are wide open and all so desiring may pay homage to the ruler's remains.

Everything, it would seem, is ready. And yet there is no sign that the move north is imminent. A week passes. Still nothing new. The truth is that the court is torn by arguments as to where and when to solemnize the wedding of the young Tsar: here in Livadia, or in the capital after the funeral. Personally Nicholas wants to be married at once in Livadia, before the funeral, "while dear papa is still with us." The Empress mother is ready to agree with this "well grounded" position, but the other members of the Imperial Family, especially the Grand Dukes, Nicholas' uncles, mute during the life of Alexander III, but now vociferous and meddlesome, are positively against such a plan. Many solutions are offered, but no one has enough authority to push a solution through.

It leaves one aghast to think that here, in this very center of unlimited power, there is no one able to cut short the inane bickering and make an authoritative decision. Two persons, however, among those present at Livadia could do so at once and not only take a firm, independent stand, but even carry out a decision without paying attention to anybody else. These two persons are the Tsar Alexander III himself and the Princess

Alice. But the former is already a corpse, while the other chooses to be silent, judging that the time is not ripe for interference.

"One must learn the difficult art of waiting." This was always one of Alice's favorite aphorisms. She has read it long ago, in England, in some educational book in her Grandmother's library, and now it helps her greatly in her tactics in regards to the affected crowd of courtiers that surrounds her.

Finally the arguments come to an end, a decision is reached. The wedding of the young Tsar will take place in the capital, after the funeral. From Livadia to Sebastopol by warship, and thence by train all of central Russia, south to north, travel the remains of Alexander III. This mournful voyage is so unusual that most of the usual precautions involved in the movement of royal trains are overlooked. Only one measure is taken—two false royal trains, one preceding the other following the train actually bearing the Imperial Family, make the trip. On the first "false" train is the body of the deceased Tsar. The mute remains no longer fear any manifestation of revolutionary terror!

***

The capital greets its dead Sovereign with damp November weather, rotting autumn fog which makes man forget the existence of sunshine. Troops line the route of the funeral procession from the Nikolaievski station to the Peter and Paul cathedral where the burial is to take place. The cortège, several miles long, opens with the passage of two knights, one in black the other in white armor. The former symbolizes grief, the latter joy for the advent on the throne of a new Tsar.

On the main street of the Capital, the Nevsky Prospect, the troops are waiting. The mournful procession approaches. A young, dandyish cavalry officer commands his squadron:

"Attention! Look lively!"

"Who is this fool?" asks one of the dignitaries, Minister Witte, future Count, who, with the other ministers is walking in front of the caisson. His colleague does not know. But the time will come when Count Witte will find out his name! The officer is Trepov, the future dictator, hero of the civil war. He is the future all-powerful General Trepov who in 1905, during the first unsuccessful revolution, will give another order, just as loud, just as clear and resonant and independent. And this order will be heard by troops all over Russia: "Don't spare the ammunition!" And the troops will obey blindly, they will suppress the 1905 revolution. Will they do it again later? Will they once more open fire against the people?…. No one among the powers that be is thinking seriously of such a contingency on this melancholy day.

The regiments spread along the streets are standing as ordered, at attention. As ordered they "look lively." Behind their even, double files there stands a thick, gray, numberless throng. Many climb on each other's shoulders, others scale trees and lampposts from where they are ordered down by the police. In the gray fog of a northern morning one can notice how the attention of this expectant crowd sharpens at the approach of the sumptuous caisson bearing the royal coffin. Behind the caisson, alone, with bowed head walks an officer, a colonel, short and unimposing. From time to time he throws timid glances around him, at the crowd.

This is the new Tsar! He does not appear as the central figure of the greatest funeral procession in history. He does not look like the majestic Emperor of all the Russias. His figure lacks the royal poise, the aura of royal grandeur.

The carriage of the future Tsarina follows. For the crowd this really is the climax of the procession. Tension mounts. Impatiently everyone tries to catch a glimpse of her straight, majestic silhouette, of her handsome face. To many this face looks morose, excessively haughty. The truth is that Alexandra is tired. A long voyage across Russia in the unfamiliar atmosphere of deep mourning and trumped-up grief, numberless requiem services, almost at every stop of the train, prolonged beyond reason by a clergy eager to appear loyal and zealous—all this has wearied the Princess beyond endurance.

But among the people, here and there, there is shaking of heads and whispers and the recurrent thought which, perhaps, has even crossed her own mind:. "She has come to us following a coffin!" The superstitious Russians could only see in this an ill omen for the new reign. And this was said about the girl who long ago, in her childhood, had been called "Sunshine" by her grandmother Victoria, Queen of England!

Exactly two weeks go by. November 14 rolls around, the day of the Tsar's wedding. The ceremony is to take place in the palace church. A special decree has removed the court mourning for that day. From early morning the Winter Palace is alive with activity. In one of the numberless halls of the palace the royal bride is being solemnly readied for the crown.

She is wearing a white silk dress embroidered with silver flowers. Her mantle is embroidered with golden ornaments in ancient Russian style. It has such a long and heavy train that five pages have been assigned to carry it. On the bride's head is a tiara of the purest and most dazzling diamonds—it picks up and enhances the young girl's pale complexion, the purity of her traits, the sparkle of her eyes.

The Tsar and groom is waiting in an adjoining hall, so-called oval room. He is wearing a scarlet hussar's uniform with golden trimmings. In his opinion this kind of uniform becomes him most. He looks happy, triumphant. His emotion is joyful for everyone to see.

But what feeling, what emotions live in the heart of the one whom the whole world considers as the luckiest of women? Here they are. The young Tsarina has revealed them with amazing candor in an intimate letter to her German childhood friend, Countess Rantzau.

"I am lonely, I am unhappy. The old illusions melt in quick succession. And where are new illusions? This mournful voyage across Russia, following a coffin? These requiem services one after the other? They make me afraid, they make me cold. And this wedding? It seemed to me like the continuation of those numberless requiems, only they had dressed me in a white dress...."

However, on this wedding day no one present is able to guess Empress Alexandra's deep, true feelings. Her face remains controlled, serene. All day it "smiles graciously" in perfect accordance with court etiquette.

Chapter 3
THE REIGN OF NICHOLAS II

The funeral is over, the wedding consecrated. Nicholas II must reign, he the blue-eyed, modest, well-mannered twenty-six-year-old who has barely come out from under the domination of a despotic father and is therefore still unaccustomed to independence.

Meanwhile the book of Fates already has spelled out the destiny of Imperial Russia. The blind whim of chance has elevated young Nicholas to the very pinnacle of the grandiose pyramid of state. The most vital interests of the huge Russian nation are henceforth bound to his every action, every movement, every word and mood.

He, the young and modest Nicholas, must forthwith, definitively and categorically solve all the problems of Russian social life. Does Russia need a Constitution? What course to take in regards to war-conscious Germany, allied France, faraway China and Japan? What does the peasant need, perennially complaining about lack of land? And what do they want, those "strange people"—the workers? And his own relatives, Grand Dukes and courtiers, all this avid, gilded crowd pressing around the throne as if waiting for something—what do they want? And the people as a whole, those countless millions chanting "God save the Tsar...." What is their need and will?

The life of many a Russian Tsar had been shattered under the weight of such problems. The iron will, the heroic fist of rulers like Peter the Great, Nicholas I, Alexander III were needed to maintain this kind of power. Which marks of the autocrat, what merits before Russia did Nicholas II possess at the time of his accession to the throne of the Empire? He had one merit only—he had been born heir to the throne. He had nothing else. He appeared even then to be destined to join the gallery of those monarchs who in all times and all countries play a role fatal to the very institution of monarchy.

***

And yet it would seem that upon mounting the throne, Nicholas II encountered everything a monarch could wish for. Russia loved at that time the idea of tsarist rule, it had faith in the new Tsar, it gave him its affection and its hopes. Everyone expected changes in the internal reactionary policies of the preceding reign, they expected amnesties, the cessation of religious and national discrimination, the end of persecutions, they hoped for trust in social forces, for broadminded thinking. Russia was tired of a regime of police repression, tired of the echoes of Alexander III's rule. Furthermore public opinion still remembered vividly the epoch of great reforms under Alexander II and the "Constitutional Charter" signed by him on March 1, 1881 which was so ruthlessly crushed by his son, Alexander III. The latter had had one justification. He had mounted the throne while still haunted by the ghastly manner of his father's death, a fact which explains to a considerable degree the subsequent emergence in his person of an embittered fanatic sworn to the principle of absolutism and reaction.

Nicholas II, when his time came, was free from any such haunting impressions. He could act with a free hand. What tender and loving appeals were sent to the young Tsar from all sides! With what eagerness the Russian people sought to find proofs that the long liberal era was finally at hand, with what a feeling of genuine exaltation did they read the words in the Tsar's first manifesto promising "to serve the welfare of his subjects"!

Nicholas moved his permanent residence to the capital and began to appear freely and unceremoniously in its streets. "He is displeased with the police," the people began to say gleefully. "He doesn't want to move around between two files of plainclothesmen!" The Emperor, it was rumored, had kindly received a delegation at Poles in spite of efforts by the Court to bar their admittance. While in London, allegedly, he had assured a Jewish group that he disliked religious and racial persecutions.

Therefore, the people argued, he is merciful and tolerant.

When Nicholas signed a document addressed to Grand Duke Serge, then Governor General of Moscow, simply as "Your loving nephew, Nicholas," the incident was noted with joy. "That's just the way he signed," the citizens enthused,

"Your loving nephew! You can tell at once he is not proud...."

The rejoicing of the liberally minded elements reached a paroxysm when Nicholas II sentenced the unpopular Chief of the St. Petersburg Police, General Von Waal, to a three-day house arrest.

"He's got his eyes open! He won't let even the police get away with anything!"

How could the rank and file of the Russian people know that the punishment officially meted for "tactlessness on the part of the Chief," was actually caused by the fact that Von Waal had fined not a simple citizen, but Countess Stroganoff, a person near to the Court, for having put out a mourning flag on her mansion before the official publication of the communiqué concerning Alexander III's demise?

And the following episode even further increased the young Monarch's popularity. One afternoon, unnoticed by the palace guards, Nicholas walked out on the Nevsky Prospect for a stroll. He was walking along the main street of the capital without attracting anybody's attention and had already covered about a mile, when suddenly he was confronted by the person of Chief Von Waal. The Chief, informed of the Tsar's disappearance, had driven in his carriage at full speed, scanning the crowd and had finally spotted the Monarch. Now he stood before him, staring at him with eyes inflamed by the icy wind and swift riding. Softly so as not to attract anyone's attention, he spoke to the somewhat startled Tsar:

"Your Majesty, this is impossible."

"But, General..."

"This is impossible, your Majesty. I beseech you to return

to the palace."

"But General, I am taking a walk."

"This is impossible, your Majesty."

This time the last words reached the crowd of passers by. "The Tsar! The Tsar!" A throng gathered, hats were thrown up in enthusiasm. The appearance of the Emperor without his retinue and guards had electrified those present. By that time, however, a number of aides had arrived and, surrounding Nicholas with a tight cordon, were taking him to the Anichkov palace, to see his mother. The dowager Empress scolded her son in no uncertain terms and he never again went to walk alone in the streets.

Simpletons and dreamers were not the only ones to express their sympathies for the young Tsar. "All our hopes are in Nicholas II, to Nicholas II goes our hurrah," the foremost liberal land and city figures toasted at their banquets. The air was literally saturated with dreams and expectations. Under those circumstances, how easily, it seemed, Nicholas II could have become a great Monarch! But did he think during those first days of his reign about what role his name would play in the history of Russia?

No one had a precise idea of what the Tsar actually did think. At first Nicholas II kept his peace. He appeared as an unknown, a knight with lowered visor, endowed sight unseen with the love of the people.

Then, on January 17, 1895, this knight finally lifted his visor. On that day at a solemn function the new Tsar was to receive delegations from the nobility, district assemblies, townships and the Cossacks who, it was known, would verbally reiterate the pressing necessity for liberal reforms. The position of the new Tsar, burdened by an ancient way of governing, was unenviable. His problem was to squelch the high hopes and dreams of the delegates with a stern, bold answering speech. This speech, this answer to those who presumed against autocracy had been prepared in advance. Here are its crucial words:

"Your foolish dreams are known to me….I shall guard the principles of autocracy as firmly and unwaveringly as they were guarded by my unforgettable parent…."

Such was the harsh reaction of the Tsar to the constitutional yearnings of the foremost elements of Russian society.

This whole occurrence bore an extraordinary aspect. The young Tsar read his speech from a text hidden inside a caracul hat which he held in his hands. He spoke so loudly, with such a high-pitched tone of voice, especially the words "foolish dreams," that the young Empress Alexandra, who at the time still understood Russian with difficulty, felt impelled to ask one of the Grand Duchesses standing by her side:

"What is the matter? What is he explaining to them?"

"He is explaining to them that they are idiots," answered the Grand Duchess. (The dialogue actually took place in French and the true words were: "Qu'est ce qu'il leur explique?" "Il leur explique qu'ils sont des imbeciles.")

One of those "idiots," one of the oldest nobility leaders from the Tver district, Utkin, was so startled by the Tsar's outbreak that he dropped a golden tray bearing bread and salt intended as a present for the Tsar according to a revered old

Russian custom. The bread rolled to the floor, the salt was spilled.

"Bad omen," murmured the stately old timers as they watched the Minister of the Imperial Court, Count Vorontsov-Dashkov pick up the gifts.

This action by Nicholas II was a gross political misstep. Never before had a Russian Tsar permitted himself to address his people in such harsh terms. Nicholas himself did not suspect that on that day history was speaking through his lips and he was taking upon himself a fatal mission carry out Alexander III's reactionary policy to its absurd conclusion and lead Russia to ruin.

Did History, did anyone care that precisely during that initial period of his reign Nicholas II was simply playing the role of a puppet-Tsar? He was an automaton, hypnotized by the influence from the upper spheres at court and king-pins of bureaucracy. He did not realize what he was doing when he carried out the alien and incomprehensible precepts of the maniacal fanatics of absolutism (still the same Pobedonostsev and Durnovo), and especially the biddings of his mother, the Dowager Empress Maria. Here is an example of what she so successfully attempted to instill into the mind of her son: "Your Grandfather, Alexander II, got it into his head to play the liberal, so he was torn to pieces by a bomb. Your father had no such ideas and, glory be to God, he passed on peacefully, like a true Christian."

This woman, so silent and quiet during the life of her stern husband, had in fact changed unrecognizably after his death, becoming energetic, meddlesome and domineering.

Meanwhile, time went on, blind and unstoppable. No one in the Imperial palace, it seemed, thought seriously about correcting the historic blunder committed by the young Tsar. The reactionary clique was too vigilant in guarding the palace doors against any liberal infiltration, against any draft or breath of true life from without.

THE CORONATION

A whole series of ceremonial functions, at the center of which stood the Sacred Crowning of the Autocrat, heralded the beginning of a new reign in Russia. According to ancient tradition this crowning had to take place in Moscow, the first capital of the Russian state.

Preparations for the Coronation of Nicholas II lasted a long time, almost a year, while members of the special Coronation Committee discussed, modified, polished and fretted over every least detail of the complex coronation ceremonial. This was a contest of prejudices, intrigues, careerism and cheap human vanity. Especially difficult was the compilation of the lists determining who was to participate in the ceremonies and what function and place each guest was to have. Awards, decoration, honors and promotions of all sorts were involved, making the task monumental.

At the same time it was necessary to redecorate and modernize the Kremlin palaces, Peter's palace near Moscow and other ancient palaces and residences that lacked modern conveniences, including electric lighting. For this purpose a monumental power station had to be built in the Kremlin itself and more than 200,000 light bulbs, not to mention miles of wiring installed. Ancient, magnificently tooled cups, goblets and platters were taken from the secret cellars of the celebrated Granovitaya Palata, the palace where as far back as in the times of Ivan the terrible the Muscovite Tsars celebrated their grandiose banquets. The priceless objects were taken from iron-bound caskets in which they had lain for centuries and lovingly, carefully, cleaned and polished.

Another problem was the election of the thrones on which the Tsar and Tsarina were to be crowned. The Tsar in person chose for himself the ancient throne of Tsar Michael, founder of the Romanov dynasty, while the young Tsarina's choice fell on the solid ivory throne of Tsar Ivan III, Ivan the Terrible's grandfather. The Empress Dowager was to use the so-called diamond throne, that same seat upon which she had been crowned on the day of her own glory, together with her husband, Alexander III. And those same diamonds would once again sparkle around her in the rays of the May sun, only this time they would be shining on somebody else's apotheosis, as the sly irony of fate had willed it, on the triumph of that very woman whom she for so long and so stubbornly had refused to recognize as her daughter-in-law.

The coach in which the young Tsarina was to ride into the Kremlin, chosen by Alexandra from among many others in the palace museum, had to be reconditioned by skilled, specialized craftsmen. This was a carriage of rare style and splendor, the masterpiece of the famous London eighteenth century coach maker Woukinall. Entirely gilded on the outside, it was topped by a golden crown with four eagles, one on each corner of the roof. The doors were ornamented with state eagles inside elaborate medallions. It had belonged to the Empress Catherine II and the young Alexandra had fallen in love with it at first sight. How can we explain such a community of tastes between these two Russian Empresses, separated in time from one another by more than a century? Perhaps the reason lies in the fact that Catherine II and Alexandra both came from far-away, poor, hopelessly provincial German towns and both had to exert a considerable amount of patience, tact and intelligence in their dealings with the scheming Russian court circles before they were able to gain positions of predominance.

Finally the preparations are completed and the ceremonial mechanism ready to function. According to tradition the Coronation festivities must begin with the grand entrance of the Imperial Couple into Moscow, following a route from Peter's palace in the suburbs, through the city and into its most ancient stronghold—the Kremlin. Hospitable Moscow had gone all out to meet its Tsar in a fitting manner. It has wrapped itself in flowers, buntings, rugs. It has erected columns and triumphal arches.

The grandiose procession moves slowly, unhurriedly, opened by representatives of the various and numerous nationalities of the Russian Empire: Turkmen, Tekins, Kirghiz, the Caucasus, the Cossacks. The Moscow crowd shows great curiosity at the sight of their exotic faces, festive costumes, tooled saddles and harness, ornate weapons.

They are followed by a long file of courtiers. Then comes

the nobility in a separate column. Then the regiment of the Guards—the Chevaliers Gardes, all of them blond, and the Gardes à Cheval, all of them dark-haired, on their powerful horses and resplendent in helmets and breast plates. Finally, at an interval from all these, alone on a magnificent, traditionally white and silver-shoed steed, the Emperor himself, Nicholas II. Young Empress Alexandra in her coach follows the carriage of the Empress Dowager who, on this day is still awarded according to ceremonial a place of preeminence.

The crowd welcomes the old Empress with such warm ovations that the latter is touched, so touched in fact that tears appear in her eyes, tears which she, for some reason, elects not to wipe off.

The route of the triumphal march lies past the small, ancient Iverskaya chapel known for centuries all over Russia for its miraculous Icon of the Mother of God. This Icon has resided here since 1684 and is one of the principal sacred shrines of the city. Here, before this chapel, comes a pathetic moment of religious humility. The Tsar and both the Empresses, symbols of unlimited worldly power, reverently bow their heads. The Tsar removes his hat. They make the sign of the cross, repeating it three times. The other participants follow their example. All, all without exception believe, and believe unfalteringly, in the miraculous power of the Icon.

Could any one have thought at that pathetic moment that years would pass and the day would come when a gang of workers would present itself before this very same shrine, sent there by a different kind of authority, that of the Soviet of

People's Commissars, to tear down the Iverskaya Icon and take it out of the city and throw it into a filthy garbage dump—"to facilitate city traffic by avoiding useless gatherings of curious citizens"?

The procession finally arrives at the Uspensky Cathedral. All the Moscow church bells are ringing. The din increases as the Tsar approaches the Cathedral. Then, at the very instant when the Tsar crosses the threshold, it ceases abruptly at a signal given by the Kremlin commandant, oddly enough with his sword. A moment of complete silence follows, broken suddenly and crashingly by the artillery salvoes of an 85-gun salute.

Here, in this very Cathedral five days later, on May 14, the religious anointment of the new Autocrat for his reign is to take place. Precisely at 7 a.m. on that date a cannon on the main Kremlin tower announces the beginning of the ceremony. It is a clear day and the warm spring sun shines brightly over the pageantry reminiscent of deeply-rooted antiquity. Trumpets and cymbals warn that the Imperial Couple has left the palace and is descending the red-carpeted steps of the so-called "Red Porch." The Tsar is wearing his Preobrazhensky Regiment uniform, the young Tsarina a gray brocade gown embroidered in ancient motifs by the nuns of the Ivanovsky monastery. The eyes of the Tsarina glisten and emotion heightens the color of her cheeks. If one is unaware that she has slept badly, awoke with a racking headache and pains in her joints—all symptoms which ever since her childhood have always accompanied stress or emotion—one could think that she is animated and happy.

Inside the Cathedral, in its very center, rises a platform atop twelve steps, bearing the Imperial throne. The Tsar and Tsarina mount the dais and seat themselves on the thrones. Two Metropolitans, sumptuously arrayed in golden vestments, follow them, bearing the ermine cape and the diamond chain of Andrei Pervosvanny, the highest order of the Empire, symbol of the might and immutability of the State. The Senior General of the Aide-de-Camp Staff carries the sacred crown of Russian Emperors, placed on a red pillow, and offers it to the Metropolitan. In a second the Tsar will lift the crown and place it on his own head. He takes a step forward, extends his hands to the crown, stops as if petrified. Something has happened, so unexpected, so unprecedented in coronation history, so somberly prophetic that all those present are thunderstruck and gape on in awe.

The heavy diamond chain of Andrei Pervosvanny, symbol of a Tsar's omnipotence, breaks or becomes unlatched and slipping from Nicholas II's chest, falls to his feet with a ringing sound. The Monarch does not move, he does not take the crown, nor lower his hands. He seems in a trance. His eyes, usually an azure-blue, widen, become empty, dimmed by a sort of leaden film. They are staring into space, beyond all surroundings into some ice-cold, bottomless vacuum visible to him alone.

A minute passes. Another. Who knows what sinister shadows fleeted before the superstitious eyes of the Sovereign in that mysterious vacuum? Was it not the finger of fate, pointing at his dynastic family, sending a nightmarish presage, even then, in that pathetic moment, demanding its atoning victim?

This leaden look in Nicholas II's eyes, fixedly staring at one point above all surrounding objects, later became well known to those state figures who had to deal with him at critical moments in the life of the Monarchy. His eyes assumed this expression under the influence of anger or of fear. Such must have been the look in Nicholas II's eyes in the last, fatal night of his life, when as an exile in far Siberia he listened to the loud and insolent voice of Commissar-executioner Yurovsky reading the merciless death sentence which was to be carried out on the spot by Yurovsky himself....

Meanwhile, at the Uspensky Cathedral, a courtier quickly picks up the glittering chain of the regalia and hands it to the Minister of Court. The Sovereign comes out of his trance. His hands move to the scarlet pillow, take the crown and raise it aloft. Following this, the Tsar personally places the Empress' crown on the head of the kneeling Alexandra. The liturgy begins and the Tsar partakes of Holy Communion inside the Cathedral altar. This concludes the church ritual of the coronation. The Imperial Couple leave the Cathedral and mount the "Red Porch" where, according to a touching tradition carried over from the times of Muscovite Tsars, they must thrice bow, bow to the gathered Russian people.

But... there is one difference between old times and the present in the execution of such a rite. Of old, the people were admitted near their Tsars, they could easily and freely see their Sovereign's bows. Not so on this occasion. Those at whom the Tsar's gesture is directed can catch a glimpse of it only through powerful field binoculars. All they can see with their naked eyes are wearisome official comings and goings, a sea of gold uniforms, banners, and the rear end of the mounted policemen's horses, pushing the crowd as far away as possible from the ceremonial focus point.

And here are other discrepancies in relation to bygone Muscovite traditions: these cannon salvoes, that Commandant silencing the bells with a wave of his sword, the Tsar personally placing the crown on his head—all this would have struck antiquity as sacrilege, insult and denigration of the sacred power of the Church.

Sovereigns of old were wont to wait until the Patriarch or Metropolitan placed the crown upon their heads, were content to ask for blessing and admonitions from the hierarchy of the Church. "Do not forget," so spoke the ancient Patriarch to Tsars waiting to be crowned, "You too have a Tsar in heaven. Be then righteous if you wish the Tsar of Heaven to be merciful towards you." But since the time of Peter the Great the members of coronation committees invariably tended to change the ritual, heavily underscoring all possible symbols of self-sufficiency, independence and omnipotence of the earthly sovereign power.

***

The Coronation at the Uspensky Cathedral ends exactly at half past one in the afternoon. The official Coronation banquet at the Granovitaya Palata is scheduled for ten after two. The peculiar architecture of this historic edifice has been left untouched throughout the centuries. The tables are set in the celebrated Vaulted Hall, scene of Ivan the Terrible's grandiose feast celebrating the conquest of Kazan, and Peter the Great's joy-making after his victory over Charles XII of Sweden.

The Coronation banquet is subject to a most complex ceremonial rite and lasts a considerable length of time. The Tsar and both Empresses sit at a special table. The guests, even the most exalted ones, must wait for the Tsar to taste the first course and, "ask to drink." The Ober Schenk then offers the Tsar some mead in an ancient goblet placed on a tray of massive gold. Only after that may the guests take their seats, having first bowed reverently with the so-called courtly bow in the direction of the Imperial table.

The right to serve the Tsar at the Coronation feast belongs exclusively to "Retired Staff officers, members of the Moscow Nobility." No professional waiters are at hand. The Ober Schenk, Count Strogonoff, has the added task of proclaiming the official toast. The ceremonial requires five toasts, one with each course, heralded by trumpets and cymbals and followed by ordnance salvoes. Here is their rigid order:

The first toast, to the health of His Imperial Majesty, is proclaimed with the sterlet course, and is followed by 61 salvoes.

The second toast, to the Widowed Empress, is drunk with the steamed lamb course and is saluted by 51 salvoes.

The third, to the young Empress, accompanies a course of pheasants under gelatin with the same number of salvoes.

The fourth toast, to the health of the Imperial Family, comes with the capons and salad. It is honored by a 31-gun salute.

And finally, in the same sonorous voice, the Ober Schenk

proclaims the fifth toast, the last one prescribed by the ceremonial order—"to all the faithful subjects," that is to all the Russian people. It is accompanied by 21 salvoes. Twenty-one and no more! It is drunk with a course of asparagus under hollandaise sauce.

Laconic and strict is the Coronation ceremonial pattern worked out by the palace employees. It admits no digression whatever.

***

It is evening. Fireworks and illumination are next on the agenda. The illumination will be touched off by the young, newly-crowned Tsarina. As an apotheosis, as a bright final accent, her gesture will symbolize earthly greatness and happiness triumphant. And in fact, all of Princess Alice's childhood dreams seem to have become a reality. She is the Empress of all Russias. Universal respect, limitless sovereign-power, the immense vastness of autocratic Russia—they are all hers. Such is the incontestable truth for everyone to see.

But what are the true, intimate feeling of the new Tsarina Alexandra? What are her spirit, her body experiencing? The constant tension of an endless day, the ceremonial kaleidoscope, brilliant but false and soulless, the bustle, the noise bear down so heavily on her sensitive nature, are so oppressive and overpowering that she feels caught in a pall of physical and spiritual exhaustion. She is afraid she will break out into tears, she fights off the menace of fainting.... She steps out on the balcony and grips the railing. Beneath her is the Moscow river and the city. She is pale, but manages to bear herself majestically straight. Training and self-control are serving her in good stead. The master of ceremonies offers her a bouquet of flowers. She touches it and the bouquet lights up. This is the signal.

At once the battlements of the Kremlin, the ancient towers, the palaces and churches blaze with multi-colored flares. The whole city is engulfed in radiance. From atop the towers powerful searchlights send shafts of electric light out into the surrounding countryside. Only one person does not see this fantasmagoria: the person who gave the signal for its beginning. Empress Alexandra has fainted and her inert body reclines in an armchair hastily brought up by a courtier.

But the palace etiquette knows how to guard its secrets well. Once again it succeeds in keeping a mournful episode from the knowledge of contemporaries.

***

Khodynsky Field is a vast expanse of land several square miles in area, situated east of Moscow, not too far from the spot where a general battle was fought in 1812 between the invading Army of Napoleon and the Russian defenders. This site was chosen for the grandiose popular festivities scheduled to celebrate the crowning of Tsar Nicholas II.

Open air theaters, circuses, carousels, swings, refreshment pavilions were erected, causing the place to assume the aspect of a gigantic fair. Prominent among other structures were picturesque tents at which the people were to receive presents in the name of the Monarch—goblets, snuff boxes, specially minted silver rubles all with the effigies of the Tsar and

Tsarina.

During the night preceding the feast, a huge multitude of people began to assemble at Khodynsky Field, coming mostly from outlying villages and towns. Towards morning the crowd had grown to perhaps half a million souls, among them women and children, packed in a mass awaiting the hour when the distribution of gifts would begin. The weather was hot, oppressive, there wasn't a breath or wind. The carbon gas exhaled by all those people remained hanging in the atmosphere, causing asphyxia and fainting among the less hardy. There came a moment when the cries of the sick caused parts of the crowd, probably out or curiosity, to move forward. In turn, the sound of voices and the motion led the outlying portions of eager gift-seekers determined not to be left empty-handed to believe that the distribution was under way. And... what happened?

The elemental surge of that immense human mass broke the wooden, shoddily assembled barriers intended to channel the queues. A number of people fell to the ground and were trampled. Suddenly, stirred by the agonized screams, the whole multitude stampeded sideways, like a herd of panic-crazed animals, and rushed with out thinking, without looking... straight at the pits!

Apparently the planners and contractors had erected the festive pavilions without a previous study of the local topography, near a series of old, long-forgotten pits which had once served some manner of geological survey.

A few short seconds later Khodynsky Field presented the following ghastly picture: shattered and upset pavilions, carousels, tents and swings and some six thousand people, in the pits or on the ground, most of them already corpses, others still screaming, begging for help. Livid, asphyxiated faces, crushed chests, bones protruding through the tatters of festive clothes. The rest of the crowd, screaming, weeping, cursing or laughing hysterically, was fleeing in all directions, indiscriminately, leaving relatives, friends, dear ones behind.

The frightful news reached Moscow by morning and by noon was known all over Russia. Only those in whose august names the festivities had been organized learned nothing at all. The highest authorities in Moscow, its Governor General, Grand Duke Sergei Alexandrovich, preferred not to sadden the radiant mood of the Sovereign Couple by an immediate disclosure of that unprecedented catastrophe.

The Tsar and Tsarina learned the tragic truth only later. It is even doubtful whether they were ever acquainted with the facts in their true, full and appalling scope. Doesn't it seem incredible that those surrounding the Tsar would not understand that by keeping him in the dark they robbed him of a chance to go directly to the people and express his compassion and grief?

Instead, a sharply negative mood was being created among the people. Some began to believe in the heartlessness of the Tsar, his indifference for the grief of his people. Others simply marked him off as "not too bright." Others still saw him born under an ill fate and spoke of the tragedy as of a bad omen for the forthcoming reign.

INITIAL YEARS

There is no doubt that in his world outlook Nicholas II was a convinced absolutist. Just as had been the case with his father, Alexander III, his whole nature was permeated with the idea that absolute sovereign power is immutable and that it is indispensable to Russia. On the other hand, he lacked the strength to promote Alexander's harsh reactionary policies against the wishes and aspirations of the socially conscious elements of the Russian nation.

First of all, the very political background had changed. Russia under Nicholas II was quite different from what it had been under his father and predecessor. Many facets of Russian life had changed so drastically with time that they required special attention and special measures for immediate regulation. Besides, everyone already knew that the young Tsar did not possess his father's iron fist. He lacked will power. He was not firm, he faltered in his convictions and decisions.

Ever since childhood he had been accustomed to obey blindly the will of his father and to acknowledge the purely feminine influence of his mother. The precepts of his tutor, General Danilovich, were also deeply etched in his mind: "Remember, Your Highness, always remember—each one of those near you is pursuing first of all his own interests." One wonders whether these words of admonition, which had greatly impressed Nicholas as a youngster, were not instrumental in fashioning the traits of suspicion and secretiveness apparent even in relation to individuals very close to his person, traits that were so characteristic of him even in the very first years of his reign.

Meanwhile the ponderous machine of the Russian State, put into motion and tested ages ago by other Monarchs, continued its dragging, monotonous routine under the new Tsar. Nicholas II, heading this mechanism, punctiliously performed all that was required of its head. In the mornings he received various functionaries and state officials—ministers, generals and other individuals bent on serving their country and pursuing their own careers. He listened attentively to their reports, signed important papers… did this day in and day out. He knew that other Tsars had done it before him, he knew above all that "Dear Papa" had done it too.

Nicholas II assumed no airs of grandeur. To the contrary he surprised onlookers by his modesty and good manners. He received visitors with reserve, but never failed in his great affability. People were positively charmed by his courtesy— especially upon first meeting him. Such a gift of being a charmer, akin to only one of his ancestors—Alexander I—was complemented in his personality by still another trait: a phenomenal memory for faces.

Even though some nuances of what his ministers had to tell him must probably have appeared ambiguous and confusing to him at first, Nicholas II listened with great absorption to their scheduled official reports. Everybody concerned noticed his talent in swiftly assimilating the gist of any problem under discussion—a talent of paramount importance to any ruler. True, even though he easily grasped what was said to him, he then often lacked the ability to isolate and select the true essence of the question.

It was easy for Nicholas II to fall under the influence of and to agree with his interlocutors. But with equal ease he could free himself from this influence, could change his conviction from one day to the next and... could break a promise given. Hence, certain state officials dealing with him suspected the Tsar of deception, cunning and even perfidy.

The politeness of Tsar Nicholas sometimes went too far, provoking annoyance and even resentment among persons devoted to him. Such was the case in the matter of deposing his ministers. Having for one reason or another decided to remove a minister from his post, the Tsar often was too embarrassed to inform him personally. This happened in connection with the Minister of Agriculture, Ermolov. Nicholas listened to a report by Ermolov with exceptional attention, and far from making any mention of retirement—a fact concerning which he, the Tsar, had already made his decision—he asked the Minister to prepare a further study on a certain matter under discussion. Ermolov returned home with no inkling that he had been removed from office. We can imagine his astonishment and indignation when one hour later he received the Tsar's order to resign.

Nicholas usually spoke without hurry, in a soft, throaty voice with a slight, barely noticeable "foreign" accent. He was wont to think carefully over every sentence, a habit that often produced awkward pauses in the conversation. Most of the time, during official business hours, the Tsar was "stingy with his words." He particularly sought to avoid arguments in which there was a chance of coming out second best, for this could undermine his prestige. For this reason Nicholas II was never in a hurry to express an opinion, preferring to keep it to himself. He did not consider this a drawback and rarely suspected that for many people it was torment to speak without getting any reaction whatever from the august listener.

The celebrated Minister of Finance Witte, and later Rodzianko, President of the Duma, related how during prolonged and vital discussions, desiring to divine the opinion of the Tsar on the matter at hand, they would try to look into his eyes in an attempt to catch at least the flicker of a reaction. But to no avail. The Tsar purposefully averted his eyes and his gaze either wandered without stopping all over the speaker's person, or simply stared into space.

We can only surmise how much the Tsar was forced to hide at the bottom of his retiring soul to pursue such tactics, and how often his pride was hurt thereby, and what suppressed anger throbbed within him, demanding an outlet.

No matter how wearisome the interviews with ministers, how taxing their reports, the work day of the Tsar did not end there. His huge desk was always piled high with important papers on which he had to write his resolutions and affix his signature until, at times, the joints in his fingers ached with fatigue. But... it was his duty to do so, for thus the other Tsars had done, thus had acted "Dear Papa." Cumbersome were the duties of a Monarch, and to Nicholas, they often seemed almost unbearable.

On the other hand, after a tedious day full of drudgery and toil, Nicholas could look forward to a comfortable armchair, delicious tea, a stroll in the park or a ride in the carriage or a sleigh, and all this in the company of "my enchanting beauty, my darling Alix." With genuine sincerity Nicholas noted in his intimate diary the common occurrences of each day. "I saw Ministers Vanovsky, Witte, Pobedonostsev. Read a lot and managed to dispose of all the backlog. Lunched later than usual because of the reception…. But spent a wonderful evening with my very dear Alix."

During such evenings Nicholas liked to play solitaire, sometimes read aloud. He delighted in sorting snapshots and pasting them into special albums. Doing so, he used a white paste sent to him from England by his cousin George V who used it for his own beloved stamp collection. The more these evening leisures distracted him from worries of state, the further they took him from the shadow of the throne, the happier Nicholas became, the more he felt and appreciated his domestic bliss. And yet, from time to time, Tsarina Alexandra could not resist touching on political themes of the day. Then the brilliant, azure-blue eyes of the Tsar would dim and he would note in his intimate journal: "A wonderful evening and ruined…."

And Emperor Nicholas II was sincere. He was a man oppressed by the complex affairs of state. These were, he admitted it himself, beyond him and did not touch him to the quick. He was genuinely and profoundly interested only in that which concerned his private family life. There is no doubt that he loved Russia with all his heart. He was devoted to Russia, wished it glory. But he carried his responsibility as a burdensome yoke. Feeling no "taste for power," he was utterly devoid of ambition and desire to succeed.

***

Every Monarch is always surrounded by scores of people spinning webs of influences, intrigues and gossip. But there are sovereigns who are strong enough to overcome, or never to feel the snares spread around by such individuals. Others became enmeshed in their strands. Emperor Nicholas II belonged among the latter. From the very day of his accession to the throne the numerous members of the Imperial Family— uncles, cousins, nephews and numberless grand duchesses and their daughters—began to lock him inside an ever-tightening golden ring.

This was a special world of "minor courts," all equipped with their own hofmeisters, schtahlmeisters and ladies bearing all sorts of complicated titles, enjoying a free and gilded way of life, not sharing the political responsibility of the "Great Court" and therefore exempt from the hourly menace of revolutionary and terrorist wrath. The men wore military uniforms, some of them serving in the Guards' Regiments, others having no connection whatever with the Army. Hardly any of them were prepared and trained for serious, responsible duty. In spite of a knowledge of foreign languages, the education level of their majority was low. Many of them showed mediocrity of mental capabilities and unmistakable signs of degeneracy.

During the preceding reigns the Grand Dukes had been totally shorn of all political influence. Now, under Nicholas II, instigated by members of their retinues, sometimes by true adventurers, and often simply by their own wives, they began to infiltrate the inner sanctum of state power. Taking advantage of their blood relationship to the manageable Monarch, they hastened to adjudicate themselves the right to meddle in social and government affairs, with particular predilection for the Armed Forces.

So here is Grand Duke Konstantin Konstantinovich, one of the Tsar's great-uncles, assuming the leadership of the Academy of Sciences as its President. True—he does write. He writes rather ungifted poetry, signing it with the initials K. R. Sometimes, in the palace theater at the Hermitage he acts, stammeringly, the role of Hamlet "in his own translation"— actually made by a nameless hired pen. Another great-uncle, Nikolai Mikhailovich, with the help of equally anonymous hands, enriches his country's historical literature with "his own" works.

Grand Duke Alexander Alexandrovich, uncle of the Tsar, becomes the undisputed master of the Navy in the role of General Admiral. Artillery, a field requiring profound and specialized knowledge, becomes the bailiwick of Grand Duke Sergei Mikhailovich, while Grand Duke Sergei Alexandrovich, former Commander of the Preobrazhensky Regiment, receives the post of Moscow's Governor General, in spite of a crying need in that area for an administrator of great talent and experience.

Power-thirsty and coarse, Grand Duke Nikolai Nikolaievich becomes Inspector General of Russian Cavalry and later Commander-in-Chief of the Guards and of the St. Petersburg Military District, Nor does Alexander Mikhailovich, wed to the Tsar's sister, ambitious but giftless, famous for his constant intrigues, wish to be left behind. He manages to promote the office of a new Ministry—"For Maritime Commerce and Ports," and nominates himself as its chief. It must be said that the life of this Ministry as an independent unit of Government was of the briefest, being abolished at the insistence of the fearless Minister of Finance Witte. The authority of Nicholas' mother—the widowed Empress Maria—stood quite apart in its significance. She had her own invisible, long-tested, sure methods of influencing her crowned son. These she applied unsparingly during the first years of his reign.

The struggle against the dilettantism and irresponsibility of these members of the royal household was too much for the responsible representatives of political power who had to tangle with them in the daily execution of their duties. Whenever a member of the Imperial Family became involved, the Tsar immediately made his Ministers aware of the difference between simple mortals and members of a reigning dynasty. One must remember that at critical moments in the life of the Nation, Nicholas II never made a final decision on the advice of his responsible collaborators alone. He always consulted one or the other among the members of his family, depending on who at that particular moment exerted the strongest influence on his mind.

Impartial time, swiftly moving, was soon to show what effects Imperial Russia and its Crownbearer suffered from the interference of less than sterling characters in the exacting task of governing the immense Russian land.

RELIGIOUS MYSTICISM OF THE YOUNG TSAR

Alexander III had been a religious man, but his piety had not gone beyond the canons and cult of the official Orthodox Church. True, he had so sought the spiritual help of Father John of Kronstadt. But Father John, though he did have the reputation of a man who heard "the voice of God," still was a perfectly legal priest.

In his youthful years Nicholas II was far from being excessively religious. But as he became Emperor, this changed drastically. It was enough to observe him during liturgy. He stood in front of everybody, never turned his head, often made the sign of the cross with a broad characteristic priestly gesture. He prayed as only persons can pray who have little confidence in themselves and seek help and guidance from above. At the end of the service Nicholas always went to be blessed by the officiating priest. Here too the ritual was strictly "ecclesiastic" in nature. They exchanged swift bows and mutually kissed one another's hand.

There is no doubt that Nicholas II's faith was above all fed by the all-encompassing conviction that a Russian Tsar is indeed anointed by God. But there were also other, more intimate and deeper psychological causes explaining his highly developed piety. There was in the life of this Sovereign something that constantly haunted his soul. Was it not the ceaseless fear for his own safety that so unbearably weighted down the Tsar's morale?

The system of protection of the Emperor and his family stood at a high level of efficiency. Night and day the palace was guarded by large numbers of policemen and plainclothesmen. Whenever the Tsar left the palace, every inch of the way was also guarded, employing the most modern and ingenious methods. And the palace park in which Nicholas liked to take an occasional stroll was also strewn with policemen disguised as gardeners, or quite openly standing on their posts as sentinels.

The persons whose responsibility it was to safeguard the Tsar's life went so far in the performance of their duty that a standing joke in palace circles related how the Chief of the "Okhrana," Colonel Kutepoff, later General, ordered the game wardens on the Tsar's hunting preserves to pull out the teeth of all the hares on the premises when it became known that Nicholas planned a hare hunt.

To a certain point the knowledge of such unfaltering vigilance may have acted soothingly on the Tsar. On the other hand it would not fail to remind him every hour that his life was threatened. No wonder then that there was something unbearably oppressive in an existence in which the thought of self-preservation dominated all others and defensive action had to remain passive, unaware of when, where and whence danger might strike.

This unescapably led to the fact that Emperor Nicholas sought sustenance in prayers. He also began to lend an attentive ear to all manner of portents and omens which seemed to have been sent as warnings from above. The next easy step was the emergence in his mind of superstition, a tendency to mysticism and engrossment in spiritualism. In turn, this threw the door wide open for all sorts of irresponsible influences from without and the Imperial Palace of Russian Autocrats, even in the first half of Nicholas II's reign, became the proving grounds for a whole series of adventurers in the field of prophecy and clairvoyance.

The most famous and influential among these, and worthy of mention was the French magician Philippe, a native of Lyons. The appearance of this man near the Imperial throne was shrouded by the most impenetrable mystery, closed to the eyes and ears of contemporaries. The French magician Philippe owed his extraordinary career at the Russian Court to two members of the Imperial Family—the Montenegro Princesses Anastasia and Militsa who had married Grand Dukes Peter and Nicholas Nicholaievich, uncles of the Tsar.

THE FRENCH MAGICIAN PHILIPPE

Short, fairly stout, a man with a modest but serious air, Philippe looked like a French school teacher dressed up for Sunday. He usually wore a black suit, quite simple, but faultlessly neat. On his neck he wore a small triangular bag of black silk containing a talisman which never left his person. Otherwise his aspect had nothing extraordinary about it if we except a pair of large, heavy eyelids weighing down over blue, caressing eyes in which burned a sort of attracting, penetrating sparkle.

On his very first visit Philippe charmed the Imperial couple to such a degree that he was immediately invited to move to Russia for permanent residence. In Tsarskoe Selo he found a house all prepared for him and, crafty Frenchman that he was, he lost no time in settling there for good. (Tsarskoe Selo was a small town in a resort area 12 miles south of the Capital. Tsar Nicholas had his winter residence there.) Once or twice a week Philippe performed feats of hypnosis, clairvoyance, incarnation and catalepsy before Their Majesties. His influence soon began to make an impression on the weak will power of the Tsar. In their protégé, besides his magic powers, Nicholas and Alexandra also valued a calm demeanor and a talent for absolute secrecy.

Having once sensed the naive credulity of the Tsar, Philippe immediately understood what advantages his combination of the pseudo-heavenly with the material could bring him in the future. Boldly he began to evoke the spirit and shadow of the deceased father of the Tsar, Emperor Alexander III, and interpret the latter's dictums concerning matters of current policy and events. This "super-natural" man, as his protectors now called him, then took the next step and began suggesting to the Tsar that there was no further need for other, earthly counselors, since he, Philippe, could keep in constant touch with higher spiritual heavenly forces. The ministers of that period noted how Philippe's influence immediately found reflection in Nicholas' outlook and in his manner of ruling affairs of State. To their astonishment they began to receive categorical orders from the Tsar on questions of highly controversial nature, with no preliminary consultation or study—an attitude that would have been inconceivable before. These sovereign decisions, as it became known later, were improvised and suggested by none other than the French conjurer.

Thus the Minister of finance, Witte, received an order to appropriate 3 million rubles from the Russian State Treasury for the King of Montenegro—father of those same two Grand Duchesses to whom Philippe owed his rise at the Russian Court. The astute Minister Witte had no difficulty in divining the underhand play of the Montenegro Princesses and he used all his influence to cut the sum down to a maximum of 250,000 rubles, incurring the great displeasure of the Grand Duchesses. The same "spirit" suddenly recommended to let the British financier Jackson build the projected subway line in the Capital. Again Minister Witte had to go all out to prove that the sum quoted in the bid was so fantastic that it surpassed by several times the actual cost of the enterprise.

***

Meanwhile information about the secret activity of the French magician at the Russian Court had reached the Chief of the Russian Secret Police in France, a man known for his vast experience, Rachkovsky, who was loath to believe in Philippe's ties with heavenly powers. Rachkovsky began his own private investigation. With the help of the French Sûreté he was able to assemble full and precise information on the past life of the conjurer. Philippe, it turned out, had his own little police and court records in France. He was by profession a butcher and had worked for many years in his uncle's butcher shop in Lyons. Meanwhile he had pursued extracurricular activities in the fields of hypnosis, healing, etc. for which he was prosecuted by French authorities.

Rachkovsky hastily dispatched this information to the Russian Minister of the Interior, Sipiagin, for transmission to the Tsar. Minister Sipiagin, a subtle and inveterate courtier, was well aware of any palace moods and decided not to "experiment" with the Monarch's feelings towards himself. He returned Rachkovsky's report to Paris with a letter in which he said the following: "I warn you that if any one ever asks me about this report of yours, I shall answer that you never wrote me anything. Answering you as a Minister I at the same time advise you as an honest man: throw this report on Philippe into the fireplace and never mention it to anybody again."

But Rachkovsky, the policeman, did not throw this report into the fireplace. He sent it now to Tsarskoe Selo, to the Palace Commandant, Hesse, who passed it on to Nicholas II. And what happened? The Emperor tore the report to pieces. At the same time the Tsar received an answer from the President of the French Republic, Loubet, denying his Majesty's request to honor Philippe with the title of Doctor of Medicine!

In spite of the French President's sincere wish to be of service to the Emperor of Russia, the laws of the Republic were too firm. However, the Council of Ministers came up with a compromise decision, Philippe would be granted the right to take examinations for a Medical Degree and it would be suggested to the examining professors to be as lenient as possible.

Having learned of this, Philippe declined "with indignation" to take the test.

But gradually the events in the palace, hidden though they

were from the ears and eyes of the general public, were beginning to impair the traditions of the Imperial Family's official prestige. Pobedonostsev, old and unshakable guardian and ideologist of absolution, began to voice his wrath.

Once, sitting at the Tsar's supper table, Pobedonostsev overheard the Tsar and the Montenegro Princess Anastasia animatedly discussing the extraordinary spiritual gifts of a provincial Bishop, Anthony. After supper Pobedonostsev approached Anastasia and started a conversation as follows:

"I've heard that you are interested even in our Bishops now. Aren't you planning to call Bishop Anthony in from Podolsk?"

"Yes," answered the Princess. "I've heard so much good about him and I would like to see him personally. You know, I have a higher instinct with which I can recognize outstanding people."

To which the old veteran of Russian absolutism answered waspishly: "It is not enough to have a higher instinct. We need a lower one as well to be able to recognize people of lower quality, to keep us from associating with unworthy individuals, adventurers it is so difficult to get rid of later on."

The Princess well understood what and who the angry Pobedonostsev was referring to. And who knows, perhaps this old man's anger was prompted by another feeling—a feeling of peevishness at the ugly fruit borne by the very seeds of absolutism he himself had so persistently nurtured and tended in the past!

The highest ecclesiastic hierarchy was also seriously perturbed by the fear that an excessive infatuation by the Tsar with occultism might undermine the authority of the

Orthodox Church in the eyes of the people. It decided to act without further delay. Bishop Theophan, personal confessor of the Tsar, took the delicate mission upon himself and began his admonishments. He enjoyed the deep and sincere confidence of the Sovereigns and finally he was able to prevail upon the Tsar to leave occultism alone. Henceforth, he exhorted, magic incantations must be supplanted by pure prayer. This, as a matter of fact, fitted Nicholas' personality much better, for incantations require will power, which he lacked, while prayer lulled and made no demands.

Father Theophan's preachings dealt the final blow to the French conjurer, who was compelled to leave not only the court but the country as well. He did not depart empty-handed, however, carrying away with him a generous share of princely gifts.

SERAFIM OF SAROV

The need for emotions of a mystico-religious character had become a constant factor in the life of the Russian Court. In tune with this mood the aforementioned two Montenegrin Princesses began to read aloud to the harried Empress—who still was somewhat shaky in her command of the Russian language—texts propounding the significance of Saints and of their relationship to God. At the same time, to the surprise of Church hierarchs, the Tsar and Tsarina expressed a passionate desire to canonize the holy Serafim, who had died in 1820 in odor of sanctity in the Sarov monastery near Tambov.

Individuals with nothing better to do had found—in the files of the Police Department of all places—a will allegedly belonging to Serafim in which he had included a prophesy pertaining to the current reign. "There will be misfortunes and national disasters. There will be unsuccessful wars. A time of great trouble will beset the land. Father will fight son, and brother will fight brother. But the second half of the reign will be bright and the life of the Emperor lengthy...." What an irony if we look today at the actual fate of the reign!

But at that time... the document excited the Tsar even more in his desire to canonize Serafim. Actually, the question of the canonization of that ascetic monk had already been extensively discussed by the Holy Synod. The statutes of the Orthodox Church, beside proof of the candidate's true righteousness during his life, also require that no less than one hundred years pass from the day of his death, and that during this period of time his body, normally buried, remain whole and untainted by decomposition. Only thus can his sainthood be recognized. The matter of incorruptibility of the flesh, in the sage conception of the Church, was considered as the chief objective sign of the supernatural, miraculous manifestation of special benevolence from the Heavenly Power.

The hundred-year anniversary of Serafim's death had not yet occurred. However, after long consultations, the Holy Synod, in view of the Tsar's pressing desire, agreed to reduce the required century time limit and finally brought forth a decree elevating the holy Serafim of Sarov to the number of Saints of the Russian Orthodox Church and ordering his body to be shown and special ceremonies to be performed in his name.

Nicholas II was overjoyed. He immediately confirmed the Synod's decree and expressed the desire that the canonization ceremonies be vested with exceptional solemnity. Preparations lasted several months. During the week preceding the holy occasion the highest prelates of the Church, thousands of priests, monks and nuns began to arrive in the little town of Sarov. They were followed by Ministers, courtiers, a mass of officials and of military figures, all desiring to demonstrate their assiduous piety before the Tsar. Pilgrims by the hundreds of thousands, invalids seeking a miracle literally submerged Sarov. The Tsar and Tsarina arrived on the eve of the celebration accompanied by singing of the Anthem, church ringing and deafening hurrahs.

Uninterrupted services were held all through the night and Serafim's body was carried three times around local churches and monasteries. The Tsar himself helped to carry the coffin containing the body of the prematurely canonized monk. Later, as it became known, the Tsar immersed himself in the small pond which had once served as bathing spot for the Saint. The following day was also marked by a series of religious ceremonies, and finally the celebration ended with the blessing of the foundations of still another church to be known by the name of the Saint.

During his life the holy Serafim had well understood the price of human vanity and had assiduously avoided people, hiding from them at times in the virgin pine forests around Sarov.

The Tsar and Tsarina left Sarov comforted by the prophecy for the second half of their reign. A year later, on July 30,

1904, Alexandra gave birth to a son—Grand Duke Alexei Nikolaievich.

***

Did the highest prelates of the Church reigning in Tsarist Russia believe in the actual sanctity of those they canonized and in the miraculous power of the icons they glorified and reverence for which was from all sides instilled into the Russian people?

There is no doubt that they did believe. However, here is a comment on this very same question, quoted from the very lips of Moscow Metropolitan Leonty.

A provincial priest, a learned man, Master of Theology, once came to see him and begged him for permission to carry the Iverskaya miraculous icon to the village of Ilyinskoe to save the life of Grand Duchess Alexandra who was hopelessly ill with childbed fever. The Metropolitan received the learned priest privately in his own rooms. He listened to the latter's entreaty, full of sincere faith in the possibility of a miraculous healing. Instead of answering, Leonty stared at the master's emblem which hung on the cassock of the priest. Then, touching it tightly with his finger, he asked in an even voice:

"What is it you have hanging here?"

"A Master's emblem, your Eminence," answered the priest.

"I see! Fine Master! It a poor scholar you must be if you believe in the miraculous power of the icons!"

Such was the simple, but eloquent and sincere answer of the topmost prelate of the Church on the question of sanctity and miraculous powers.

***

Many phenomena of Russian national life, many facets in the behavior of Russian Tsars can not be fully understood without throwing light at the profound significance the Orthodox Church had for every Russian in the past. From time immemorial, from the very day on which the name of the Russian people appeared on the pages of history, not a single act of any importance in the life of the State and of the private individual was ever performed in that land without the participation of the Orthodox Church. It was a part of the Russian people's lives, it permeated them with its magnificent ceremonial rites, with the influence of its immovable dogmata, with the influence of its hierarchy. It had complete control over the visionary Russian soul, over the hearts and imagination of the people.

The faith of a Russian, if we look deeply into his consciousness, was perhaps simple and naive, poor in intellectual and theological elements, but full of visions, deep mysticisms and superstition. Hence his belief in miracles. A personal intervention of Deity into the affairs of men in no way struck him as unnatural, rather seemed quite admissible.

It seemed that nothing, no external factors would ever be able to snuff out in the soul of the people this mystical faith in the supernatural power of Deity.

And the faith of the Tsar differed but little, in its essence, from the faith of the people....

REACTIONARY POLICIES IN THE GOVERNMENT

Meanwhile, outside the powerful walls of the Imperial palace, the huge bureaucratic apparatus of the Russian State, set into motion by Peter the Great, continued its daily monotonous work without changing rhythm. It moved out of inertia, ponderously, monotonously, but so far without interruptions. But how long could the huge ship of state move by inertia alone, without the firm hand of an experienced pilot? No one at the time stopped to consider upon what social factors the Tsarist rule was based. It was assumed that the young ruler had inherited not only the throne, but its foundation as well, and that so long as no tremor was noticed in the throne, there was no need to worry about the foundation.

Neither the Tsar, nor his collaborators, had in their minds any precise political goals or any definite government program. The inviolability of the basic laws assigning to the Tsar the exalted position of a "chess King," dictated every move. It was suggested to Nicholas II mainly by an instinct of self-preservation and he strove to preserve the existing order of things with even greater alacrity. For this reason, from the very beginning of his reign, he entrusted state power only to individuals who fully shared the same views and ideas.

***

The Minister of Interior appointed by the new Tsar, I. Goremykin, was characteristically representative of such a type of person. Retrograde by conviction, bureaucrat from head to toe, Goremykin was concerned above everything else with the protection of his own interests. There have been attempts to ascribe him a reputation as expert on the peasant question, so important a factor in the life of the Russian people. Of course this reputation was exaggerated.

Goremykin felt little interest or sympathy for the unfortunate economic status of the Russian peasantry. According to people who knew him intimately, he was a ladies' man and inordinately proud of his beautiful growth of cheek whiskers. It was related in palace circles that this sly courtier, doubting the solidity of his position, once threw a masterful fit of simulated hysteria in the Emperor's private study. Frightened, the Tsar began to console the old man, gently stroking his hands, and after that favored him with his personal gracious disposition for a long time to come.

Finally, however, Goremykin fell into the net spread for him by the much smarter and subtler Minister of Finance, Witte, and was deposed quite unexpectedly for himself. He learned about it during a trip abroad from a newspaper he was reading at some small railroad station.

The question of finding a substitute for the political post of Minister of the Interior, so important in Tsarist Russia, was not an easy one. Many facets of Russian life had become highly involved and required great foresight in their regulation. The choosing of ministers, one of the really important prerogatives of sovereign power, always put Nicholas II in a very difficult position. The Tsar was too little in contact with life, with real people to perform this duty efficiently. And yet it as precisely here that neither routine nor the inertia of a bureaucratic machine could be of any help. The Tsar had to show his own initiative in selecting the highest statesman of the land.

With sadness in his voice the young Tsar turns to a man made wise by a long experience in affairs of state, K. N. Pobedonostsev: "How difficult it is, Konstantin Petrovich, to find an honest and suitable candidate for Minister of the Interior."

"Whom do you have in mind, Your Majesty?" asks Pobedonostsev.

"Either Plehve, or Sipiagin. Which of the two would you advise me to appoint?"

"One is a blackguard, the other a fool," answers the old ideologist of autocracy in these very words, with a sigh.

This was a harsh endorsement. And who was appointed? Both in turn—Sipiagin first, then Plehve.

***

Whether Pobedonostsev was right in his sharp opinion of Sipiagin, chronologically the first appointee as Minister of the Interior, the latter was a man of great means and a great lover of the hunt. He often participated in the Tsar's hunting expeditions, producing a certain effect on the Monarch—a fact that led to his elevation.

Under his leadership reaction openly became a doctrine of the State. In all fairness we must say that Sipiagin did undertake a revision of agrarian laws, but the results took a long time in coming. Meanwhile, as direct consequence of the government's reactionary tendencies, the internal social forces of the land continued to develop and the flames of public discontent began to lap here and there at the edges of the bureaucratic structure.

Student unrest began to be noted in several large Russian cities and gradually assumed the proportion of open demonstrations hostile to the government. The Minister of Public Education Bogolepov took punitive measures against such students in the form of compulsory military service for the mutineers. The assassination of the Minister by a student, Karpovich, was the answer to that progressive measure. It was characteristic for the political climate of the time that neither the assassination of the Minister, nor other excesses provoked any criticism or protest in the broad circles of population and in the press.

The activity of Sipiagin as Minister of the interior lasted only a short time. He fell victim of a pistol shot fired at him by a young man named Balmashev. The latter had disguised himself in the uniform of the personal aide-de-camp to Grand Duke Sergei Alexandrovich, Governor General of Moscow, and was able to imitate the demeanor and characteristics of a man of that station so well that he immediately won the trust of the guards around the Ministry and of the Minister's private secretary. The disguised terrorist was admitted to the Minister's study, allegedly to deliver an urgent secret message of great importance. Immediately after firing the fatal shot, Balmashev surrendered himself to authorities. He was tried according to martial law and was sentenced to death. The trial disclosed that he was a young man carried any by political ideals who had decided to sacrifice his own life for his convictions.

A heartfelt petition for mercy was received by the Minister

of Justice and had to be forwarded to the Tsar. The Minister of Justice at the time as Manukhin, a man of great humanity. He decided to submit the petition to the Tsar at what he thought would be the time most propitious for the condemned man's fate. For this, Manukhin took advantage of the days preceding Easter. Here precisely he chose Holy Friday, immediately at the end of the religious service which on that day is particularly permeated with the spirit of Christianity.

What did the efforts of the humane Minister lead to? They were vain. "No. I am not going to forgive him for Sipiagin," Nicholas answered briefly, calmly, without the least tremor in his. voice. This refusal dropped as a heavy stone on Manukhin's heart and from then on he did not conceal his doubts about the kindness and mercifulness of Nicholas II, so often ascribed to him by many.

***

As if Sipiagin's death had long been expected, a decree was published the very next day, appointing Plehve Minister of the Interior. Apparently the Tsar's decision concerning Plehve had been ripe for a long time, Pobedonostsev's unflattering report notwithstanding. The new Minister, it must be admitted, was one of the most colorful political figures of that period.

Of plebeian origin, Plehve always harbored a hatred for nobility, for all sorts of social and palace conventions. There is no doubt that he stood much higher than the individuals surrounding the Tsar, mainly because he possessed a strong will power which he was able to use quite fearlessly. Plehve's policy was a new turn of the governmental rudder against the progressive current of Russian life. Plehve did not want to peer into the distant future. Posterity did not interest him. He set up as his immediate political problem the preservation of the existing order. He well understood that the needs of a multimillion nation, constantly evolving and increasing on the huge territory of Russia, were so complex that they would require a reforming genius for their solution such as it was useless to expect under existing conditions. Therefore he excluded from his policy any plans for the satisfaction of these needs.

Above all the new Minister strove to paralyze, or at least slow down the ever-increasing process of infiltrating of the popular masses by anti-governmental and anti-dynastic ideas which could lead to an open revolution. This is why Plehve became particularly inimical towards all conscious strata and classes of the population and their activities. He became an open foe of town and country autonomous administrations, of any kind of associations social, professional, or even scientific. Censorship over the printed word rose to the highest point of strictness under Plehve.

Another question of paramount importance, pushed to the fore by the spectacular development of heavy industry in Russian life, the workers' question, also felt the brunt of Plehve's myopic, aggressive policy.

The whole administrative apparatus of power was in Plehve's hands thanks to the centralized system of rule that acted as a silent, obedient spring transmitting to the remotest corners of Russia every whim and nuance of his powerful will. In this manner the omnipotent Minister was sure he would be able to preserve his own order of things. Is it strange then that with a similar system of rule all the conscious elements of the population became more and more rabid enemies of the government?

But did the political course adopted by Plehve earn approval with Tsar Nicholas II? At any rate the Monarch showed no patent resistance to its development. Plehve himself once, presumably in a slip of the tongue, let out a characteristic phrase, as reported by a Professor of the St. Petersburg university, Yanshul, a close friend of the Minister: "You know, the most right of all rightist reactionaries in our Government is the Tsar himself."

Plehve personally was far from being a coward. He was perfectly aware that in promoting such a provoking, aggressive policy, he put himself, his very life, under a menace which could not be averted even by the most alert protection that surrounded him day and night. For this reason he was fond of conditioning all his promises and appointments with the significant phrase: "Provided I am still alive."

Nor was Plehve afraid of the clouds that were swiftly approaching over Russia from the East in the shape of an ever-increasing threat of war against Japan. As many other figures surrounding the Emperor, he welcomed this war as a saving valve, a device that would convert the accumulated, hostile energy of the opposition into "free steam." Of course he believed in an easy victory of Russia over Japan. At times Plehve was forced to argue with people who held less optimistic views concerning a Russian victory in the forthcoming war. Then the Minister was fond of confronting his opponents with the following reasoning: "It is just a question of simple arithmetic. A ratio of 150 to 59." Plehve referred to the difference in population between Russia (150 million) and Japan (50 million) and with this single calculation determined Russian chances for certain victory.

The events of a quickly approaching future were to show how sometimes statesmen can err, how wrong were the "all-seeing" Plehve and his collaborators in the evaluation of their enemies, both internal and external.

WAR AGAINST JAPAN

General Kuropatkin, who in the first years of the new reign occupied the post of Minister of War, certainly was a man standing in close contact with the Tsar at the most varied moments in the life of the State. Not without surprise, he informed Count Witte of the grandiose imperialistic plans for the future flourishing in the mind of Nicholas II. Conquest of Manchuria, annexation of Korea, taking of Tibet—all this entered into the plans and dreams of Nicholas II. He thought it would be particularly profitable to entice the Japanese into Korea because "it is better to fight them on the Korean mainland." He also dreamed of taking Persia, seizing the Bosphorus and even the Dardanelles. The Tsar, it seemed, was lavishly rewarding himself in his fantasies of a future time for the reverses that plagued him in the present.

Difficult and thankless was the role of his Ministers, especially the Minister of Foreign Affairs, who naturally could not approve of a policy involving such risky adventures. The Minister had to use unflagging tact and efforts in pointing out to the Tsar all the dangerous consequences connected with his aggressive ideas. Nicholas II would listen, silent and unprotesting, as though agreeing with the peace-loving arguments of the Minister. But this was only a tactic. In his secret thoughts the Tsar believed that he, as Monarch, in ultimate analysis could understand Russia's true problems better than any minister.

This is why any casual, irresponsible favorite, willing to yes the Tsar's plans in a servile manner found himself in a much more advantageous position and was able by his yessing to acquire trust, influence and even to "manipulate" the Tsar. In precisely such a position of lucky favorite at this time we find a certain Bezobrazov. The influence he exerted on the Tsar had fatal and incalculably woeful consequences for the future of Russia. The country was dragged into an unsuccessful war against Japan.

The Minister of Foreign Affairs, Count Lansdorf, and the Minister of Finance, Witte, warned the Tsar, but to no avail. At a distance of eight thousand miles everything appeared in a reduced perspective to the eyes of the Emperor and of his entourage—sluggish, submissive China, faceless Korea, the tiny islands of Japan, populated by short, ugly people. How all of this paled before the battle history of the "Victorious Russian Armed Forces," before the unencompassed vastness of Russia, before the brilliance of the Tsar and the glitter of his Court!

Japanese representatives attempted to ask for explanation of the Russian activity in the Far East, first contacting the Russian Vice Roy, Admiral Alexeiev, and then taking the matter directly to St. Petersburg. The answers they received were so unsatisfactory that they convinced Japan even further of Russia's far-reaching aspirations. Meanwhile the Eastern-Chinese railroad was being completed and feverish efforts were being made to fortify the Russian stronghold of Port Arthur. Nobody doubted in Russian ruling circles that Japan would never risk a war and that if it did risk it, it would certainly lose. Certain reactionaries, headed by Plehve, even thirsted for a "safe" clash with Japan. The column of absolutism, they argued, would be embellished with easy laurels and the bayonets of a victorious Army would put an end to revolt and revolution.

And so the fateful day arrived, January 26, 1904. At night, while the position lights of the Russian line ships glowed in the bay at Port Arthur, three Japanese destroyers silently approached and launched their torpedoes into the flanks of the "Tsesarevich," "Retvisan," and the "Pobeda." Thanks to their good construction, the ships did not sink, but they were put out of commission for a long, long time.

Thus began the Russo-Japanese War.

On the following day there was the usual reception in the Tsar's Palace. A guest began to speak with a sad expression about the tragic loss of Russian warships at Port Arthur. Nicholas II answered casually: "I consider that no more than the bite of a flea."

And in fact, during these days, Nicholas astonished his entourage with his unconcerned attitude towards the developing drama, "We will smother the Japs with our hats," shouted the stupid, servile chauvinists, seconding the Tsar's optimism.

Nicholas calmly continued to live within the current interests of his personal life, his own distractions, doggedly avoiding all that was unpleasant, serious, all that one would think should have provoked in the Monarch a natural sense of alarm.

General Rydzevsky, acting Court Minister, met the Tsar one hour after the news had come announcing the death at Port Arthur of the best Russian Admiral, Makarov, and the loss of the flagship "Petropavlovsk."

"It's been a long time since we haven't hunted together," the Tsar said, smiling. "What wonderful weather. How nice it would be to hunt a little today."

Embarrassed by the unexpected nature of such a remark, Rydzevsky did not know what to answer. Shortly after that the General personally saw the Tsar, armed with a small hunting rifle, shooting crows. Nicholas even considered it necessary to note the results of this hunt in his intimate journal: "Today I killed two crows."

There rises from the night of eternity, begging for comparison, the historical image of King Louis XVI of France who marked days without a hunt with the notation, "Nothing today," even though on these very days he was unable to go hunting only because Paris was on fire with revolutionary outbursts that already shook the foundations of his throne.

But what were the true feelings of Nicholas II at such moments? Certainly it would not be simple indifference for his country's interests. Was it not perhaps the sensation of his own inability to change the tragic reality? He seemed to shut his eyes against the terrifying images on the stage of reality, vaguely understanding that they were only the prelude to a drama in which his personal participation would become unavoidable.

The whole course of the Japanese war consisted of a series of reverses. To the Tsar they appeared as isolated episodes. But in reality the Russian Army suffered serious defeats at Liaoyang and Mukden. Port Arthur fell. Finally, in the naval battle of Tsushima, practically all the Russian fleet was destroyed. Inside of Russia these events were beginning to show their effects. From a state of indifference towards military successes, Russian public opinion awakened in great excitement. Voices proclaiming that it was time to put a finish to the senseless war, to bloodshed and shame began to be heard louder and louder, bolder and bolder at meetings and in the press. And in fact, the war had uncovered great defects in the Government, not only in military, but in civilian matters as well.

The second half of 1904 brought forth a rash of events that pointed at the existence of a truly revolutionary ferment. Minister Plehve was assassinated. This was an irreparable blow against autocracy, for in Plehve it lost its fighting and idealistic leader. News of agrarian disorders began to arrive. Peasants were burning landowners' houses. Unrest spread to the workers and more and more often the Government had to call out the troops to restore order. This provoked still further irritation, fanning the population's hatred against troops and the Government.

In Moscow, in the middle of the day, an exploding bomb killed the Governor General, Grand Duke Sergei Alexandrovich, uncle of the Tsar and hated by the citizens he had governed.

These ominous symptoms of an approaching revolutionary storm, sharply brought before the Tsarist Government the need of ending the disastrous war at the earliest possible moment. At that very time, the President of the United States of America, Theodore Roosevelt, addressed himself to the Russian and Japanese Governments with his historic offer to mediate a cessation of hostilities and a conference for the conclusion of peace. Both the Tsarist Government and Japan agreed to accept President Roosevelt's peace offer. The town of Portsmouth was selected for the conference, S. U. Witte was named Chief of the Russian Delegation. The choice of that truly great Russian statesman was most fortunate. Russia's position at the peace conference appeared very difficult and demanded consummate leadership.

Witte fully justified the trust given in him, showing his extraordinary political and diplomatic talents in all their scope. An agreement between the two countries was reached, war liquidated and a peace treaty signed on terms not ignominious for Russia. In spite of the military defeats, Russia did not have to pay a single ruble in reparations and only ceded to Japan its concessions in Korea and China and the southern part of Sakhalin Island which once upon a time had belonged to the Japanese. Witte's diplomatic merits were recognized all over the world and he was awarded the title of Count by Tsar Nicholas II.

***

Meanwhile, in Russia, neither peace, nor the nomination of the liberal Prince Sviatopolk Mirsky as Minister of the Interior in place of Plehve, victim of assassination, nor the partial liberal measures undertaken by the Government were able to calm or satisfy the minds of the Russian people. Events precipitated, bringing forth symptoms of ever-increasing gravity. Russia was entering a new period in its history—the revolutionary period.

Student youth and workers were staging open demonstrations. Street manifestations with banners and posters covered with slogans hostile to autocratic government became a common occurrence. They were accompanied by the singing of revolutionary songs such as: "Working people, arise and unite!"

The shouts and songs of the crowd reached the windows of an old two-story house in the very center of the Capital where the ancient ideologist of absolutism, K. Pobedonostsev was living out his last days. The din reached the ears of the eighty year-old patriarch, but they did not provoke his answering anger. He was completely immersed in prayer and in scholarly research. The revolutionary melody died out before those ancient Russian sacred chants that filled his soul.

And when representatives of the infuriated mob attempted to penetrate inside his house, Pobedonostsev, with a hand already cold with approaching death, proffered at his "friends and foes" a small volume on whose cover one could see the inscription: "New testament of our Lord Jesus Christ—in a new translation by K. P. Pobedonostsev." In this "Testament" he saw the true freedom of an individual's soul.

There was an element of historic tragedy in this helplessness of a man descending into his grave from the arena of life, made wise by a tremendous experience in the ways of men and governments, who in those far away March days of the year 1881 had played such a decisive role in the history of his country.

And the howling mob left the old man alone and continued its triumphal march glorifying those same principles to which Pobedonostsev had once dealt such a blow.

Meanwhile, events were getting out of hand. Members of various professions began to group into unions bearing a purely political character. A union of printers was formed, followed by a union of postal and telegraph workers, railroad workers, metallurgists, engineers, lawyers, etc., etc.

The idea arose of combining all these politico-professional unions into one powerful union of unions—a feat which eventually was achieved. The general unrest and excitement in the country could not go on without provoking an approving echo in the Army and the Navy, especially among the enlisted men.

The preparations for a general strike were in full swing. Everything was mobilized for the conquest of political freedoms and popular representation. All social forces in the land were put into action. Finally, on October 10, 1905, this general strike, unique in history for its immeasurable scope, paralyzed a territory covering one sixth of the globe. Both Russian capitals—St. Petersburg and the ancient Moscow—as well as all Russian cities and towns went dead. There was darkness in the streets at night. The provinces were cut off from the cities. All transportation and communication broke down. The mails, the telegraph and telephone were idle. Food supplies ceased to flow to the markets.

The breath of the revolutionary beast was felt everywhere.

Panic seized the Court and the Government. Nicholas II was weathering the crisis in Peterhof, not far from the Capital, communication with which could be had only by boat.

There was no doubt that Tsarist power and the dynasty stood face to face with the menacing danger of their downfall. And here once again the experienced hand of a seasoned pilot came to the rescue. Without losing a second, Count Witte prepared a manifesto proclaiming the granting to the Russian people of all civil and political freedoms and the institution of people's representation in the form of a new legislative body, the State Duma.

Witte urgently took this charter to Nicholas II for his signature. On the night of October 17, Tsar Nicholas II signed the manifesto.

Count Witte's calculation was justified.

The Imperial Manifesto, composed as everybody knew by the hand of the popular statesman Witte, had its immediate effect. The elemental forces of the revolutionary storm lost some of their fury. The general strike ended. True, complete calm did not come for a long time. But the Government had managed to grasp control over the events. Scattered disturbances, isolated revolts were dealt with by military force. In the Capital, similar flare-ups were quickly extinguished by

General Trepov.

Thus, with a sharp twist of a hand on the rudder of the ship of State, Count Witte was able to veer off the path of revolution onto that of evolution at the very last moment of impending doom. Russia was led out onto the broad and straight constitutional road. Now it would be the task of future Tsarist leaders to hold the course of salvation indicated by the new manifesto.

The merit of Count Witte before Russia and particularly before its Tsar and the whole dynasty was incalculable. How did Tsar Nicholas II thank Count Witte for this service?

The feeling of gratitude does not belong to all Monarchs. Count Witte fell into disgrace and soon was forced into retirement. Tsar Nicholas II did not like him, as he disliked all people with a strong mind will power. The Tsar felt uneasy with people of that sort. Bismarck would not have lasted long with Nicholas II!

The Emperor showed his dislike for Witte even after the latter's death. How could that come to light?

Count Witte left a will in a heavily sealed envelope with a letter addressed to Emperor Nicholas II. Immediately after Witte's death, this letter was forwarded to the exalted addressee. Here is the content of that letter:

Your Imperial Majesty:

These lines will reach you, my Sovereign, when I will be standing before another Throne.

I address you now with a request from my grave.

No matter how contemporaries judge the

present, impartial history will enter into its books your great deeds for the good of the people.

[Five lines are here omitted. They were a detailed resume of all the services rendered to his country by the late Count.]

What the Russian people will never forget, so long as there will be a Russian Nation, is that Emperor Nicholas II called his people to participate in the legislation of the land.

This is your merit before the Russian people and humanity. Historians, exalting your deeds, will also mention your collaborators among whom was Witte. As reward for his merits before you and the fatherland you have elevated him to the rank of Count.

All-merciful Sovereign, give this title of count to my beloved grandson, Lev Kirilovich Naryshkin. Let him be called Naryshkin, Count Witte. [Count Witte had one daughter who, marrying Naryshkin, lost her maiden name and her title. Since Witte had no other children, his title, even though hereditary, was to become lost after his death.]

I shall not burden you with an explanation of my family situation. I shall only say that I love this boy only as a grandfather can love his grandson.

For such a kindness I shall constantly pray to the Almighty in the other world for the well-being of you and your dear ones.

Be happy, my Sovereign. May Christ keep you.

Your servant, who was faithful always and at all times.

Count Witte—now praying God for you.

Tsar Nicholas read this petition by Witte, but left his request from the beyond without satisfaction.

In his secretive soul the Tsar could not find enough kindness nor gratitude towards the memory of the greatest statesman of his epoch.

Without saying a word to any one, in silence, the Tsar hid this letter into the remotest corner of his archive.

TSARINA ALEXANDRA AND HER ENTOURAGE

PRINCE ORLOFF, ANNA VYRUBOVA

The story-book wealth and luxury surrounding the absolute rulers of the Russian Empire played an important role in the life of the young Princess Alice during her first visit to St. Petersburg. This display of glitter made a deep and permanent impression upon her sensitive adolescent soul.

And now, in her turn bearing the crown of a Russian Tsarina, she glories in this feeling of omnipotence from the very first days of her reign. This can be noticed in the way she treats her entourage, in the way she carries herself, in her correspondence.

Tsarina Alexandra actually knew little about Russia. Her English tutors and teachers had not told her much about that "half-savage" country, that huge plain inhabited by a retarded, ignorant people with needs and aspirations so remote and hard to understand. In the mind of the German Princess the art of living and ruling in such a country appeared greatly simplified. She had conceived the Russian state as something primeval, as it had existed two centuries earlier in the epoch before the reforms. She had no intention of modifying her views—nor did she modify them to the very end of her reigning days.

"You and Russia are one and the same," she kept repeating to her crowned consort. "No one has the right to forget this and to usurp your rights."

It must be said, however, that during the first years of the reign the influence of the young Tsarina on the course of Russian political affairs was not noticeable. Nicholas II resented her attempts to meddle in government matters. She realized that and temporarily desisted from any interference in order to avoid misunderstandings with her husband.

During that period all political influence belonged to the mother of Nicholas II, Empress Maria, the very woman who had at first forbidden Nicholas to marry Princess Alice. But Alexandra was not one of those persons who can step back, submit to circumstances and become simply a "silent one"—as more than one had done in the long chain of Russian Tsarinas.

"One must be able to master the difficult art of waiting." Alexandra had long adopted this principle as a golden rule of life. And now she decided to wait. She realized it was impossible to storm the "fortress." She could not foretell on whose side the balance of power would be—on the mother's or on the wife's side? She remembered how Nicholas had once obeyed a whim of his mother and had so easily abandoned her, Alexandra, the woman he loved.

It was necessary to wait, wait for an alienation between mother and son, wait for the passionate and ever-growing love of a husband for his wife to flare even stronger, and then... the weak, vacillating will of the Tsar perhaps might be bolstered, substituted by her own will.

But there was in the life of the Tsarina something that worried her day and night. It was fear. She admitted that she was afraid of revolutionaries. Actually she was much more afraid of an inside, palace revolution or coup.

"How the profile of your husband resembles the profile of Emperor Paul I." These words, uttered jokingly by the Prince of Wales in London during a lunch celebrating her engagement had profoundly imbedded themselves in the memory of Tsarina Alexandra. The terrifying ghost of Emperor Paul, suffocated by his own courtiers, often and persistently tortured her soul.

The Palace Commandant, following her instructions, issued new orders, strengthening the palace guard, not only on the outside, but on the inside as well, in the halls and passages, even by the doors of the Tsar's and Tsarina's bedroom. According to the new disposition the sentinels were ordered to shoot without warning at any unknown person found in an unauthorized place or at the wrong time of day or night.

But Paul, that unbalanced Tsar, Alexandra seemed to reassure herself, was to blame for what happened, he trusted people too much. He trusted ministers, generals, Grand Dukes, he trusted that false, flattering, servile crowd of courtiers. It is necessary to know how to find true friends one can depend on. The Tsar must not trust everybody—to the contrary, he must suspect all. Tsarina Alexandra knew only too well the worth of the intrigue-loving, eternally bowing swarm of court retainers around the Russian throne. The memories of her sojourn in Peterhof when, as a naive young girl she had tortured herself in doubt—would they accept her as a suitable fiancée or not?—these memories now persecuted Alexandra like a painful nightmare. She remembered how the slavish courtiers had been quick to sense her reverse and how they had immediately changed their attitude in her regard.

There had been but one man who had not faltered and had even seemed anxious to compensate for the tactlessness of the others. She had remembered him well—the impressively handsome officer of the Gardes à Cheval, Prince Orloff. There was a man she could trust, there was a hand upon which she could lean.

***

Tsarina Alexandra Theodorovna recognized Orloff on the very day of the coronation, picking him out in the long file of mounted troops. She smiled at him joyfully, nodded her head at him, and even waved her hand, thereby breaking the rigid etiquette of the coronation ceremonial.

A month later Orloff was named Aide-de-Camp to Their Imperial Majesties. Then, following the wish of the young Tsarina, he was made Commander of the Lancers' Regiment, honorary Commander of which was Alexandra herself. And soon he received the rank of Major General of His Majesty's retinue.

Tall, well-built, handsome, with a charming, somewhat melancholy smile, intrepid cavalryman, winner in more than one equestrian competition, Orloff belonged to that closed circle of St. Petersburg nobility where no one envied wealth for everyone was wealthy, and where no one played up to other people's influence because influence belonged to all. It was nothing extraordinary in that circle to be on terms of close camaraderie with the Tsar, or to marry the daughter of a Grand Duke, as had been done by Count Stroganoff and by Prince Mukhransky-Yusupoff.

However, even in those circles, Orloff's meteoric rise, his nearness to the Imperial Family, provoked a good share of astonishment, rumors, gossip. This gossip annoyed, maddened Orloff. To get away from its pressure he had recourse to strong drink, cocaine and other narcotics. But he was powerless to stop the vicious talk.

The favorite pastime of the Tsar and Tsarina was cruising in the Baltic Sea and the Finnish Fjords on the Imperial yacht "Polar Star." Orloff always accompanied the royal couple on these trips that were regarded strictly as entertainment and during which an informal atmosphere reigned aboard the yacht, without court etiquette, without ranks and order of precedence. The autocrat disappeared. The Tsar became a hospitable, kind, generous host.

The company on the "Polar Star" was not numerous. Usual guests were the Minister of the Navy, Admiral Birilev, a few Aides-de-Camp, the Court Reader, Mme. Schneider, and the Lady in Waiting, Princess Orbeliani. After a late, tasty supper, the Tsar usually went on deck and there, stretched out on a chaise, he liked to listen, often laughing uproariously to Jewish jokes ably and assiduously told in turn by Admiral Birilev and Aide-de-Camp, Prince Obolensky.

Orloff introduced a certain dissonance into this group. The gay laughter of the Tsar and of the diligent raconteurs did not find an echo in Orloff's melancholy mood. His regal calm, his controlled courtesy were as noticeable to all as his imposing physical appearance. Near him Admiral Birilev appeared as an old man's caricature, Obolensky as a dandified figure and the Tsar himself seemed short and homely.

And only Tsarina Alexandra among all those present could be a match to him in beauty, stature and regal carriage. On evenings like that she liked to sit at the piano and play Beethoven, whose sonatas she had learned to perfection as a girl. Inspired, her fingers wandered over the keyboard and suffused the melodies with their own, mysterious sensuousness. Orloff would sit in a corner, gazing sadly but deeply and persistently in the direction of the piano, attempting to interpret its sounds as sentiments which perhaps he was unable to hear uttered in plain words.

For a long time the Tsarina had yearned for a friend, for a woman companion with whom she might be sincere and at ease. And the lips of Prince Orloff pronounced the name: Anya Taneieva. He suggested that the Empress invite her to the yacht. Did Orloff realize that in giving this advice he was taking an average Russian girl and creating the future Vyrubova (the Empress got Anya Taneieva married off to Vyrubov, a naval officer), that "best friend of the Tsarina," that court favorite destined to play a role so fatal to Imperial Russia and to the Dynasty?

***

Plain, even though rosy-cheeked and tall, but clumsy and with a heavy figure, Anya Taneieva, even as a girl, had resorted to all sorts of stratagems to catch the attention of the Empress. In this endeavor she showed a purely catlike cunning, walking for hours in the park at Tsarskoe Selo in the hope of meeting the Tsarina and bowing to her to the waist.

Her father, Taneiev, occupied the high but purely bureaucratic position of Chief of His Majesty's Chancelry. He reported to the Emperor on regularly appointed days. Through him Anya managed to send handicrafts of her own making as gifts to the Tsarina. The latter sent word of thanks, but soon forgot the incident. Anya was invited to the palace balls together with other girls of her station, but was unable to attract special attention.

Later she even received the title of Lady in Waiting of her Majesty. The Tsarina personally gave her the medallion required by Court Etiquette, but still did not show any particular interest in the girl. All this was too far removed from the goal of Anya's ambitions. And it seemed that nothing promised a change for the better.

***

And then the family of the Chief of His Majesty's Chancelry was suddenly plunged into joyful confusion. A letter from the Tsarina arrived, asking that Anya be allowed to come to the yacht for an excursion into the fjords.

The old Taneiev could not for the life of him guess to whom he owed such an exceptional honor. This was more important than any bureaucratic award. This is a path to the very hub of power. And the father hovered over his daughter, choosing the best luggage, even helping her to pack. It suddenly seemed as if he were actually seeking her favor now that she had been touched by the finger of fate!

Anya was met cordially on board the yacht. "You now have a subscription to take these trips with us," the Tsar told her smiling. And Anya did not know what to answer, her limbs were frozen from emotion.

But she was quick to recover. Even then, with the flair of a hysterical woman, she could sense how close she was to winning. Though haughty by nature, the Tsarina was also simple and sincere. She was proud, but very lonely and powerless to avoid the nets of false adoration, simulated devotion which "her best friend" Anya was preparing to cast. And so the Imperial yacht, the Empress, Orloff, they all stand before Anya Vyrubova. And in the still unfathomable perspective of the future there loom Tsarakoe Selo, Rasputin and… the whole chess board of autocratic power. Anya will not forget this. She is deeply appreciative of the service Orloff has done her.

Orloff's star rose like a brilliant, swift meteor. It fell in an equally swift and unexpected manner. Orloff died suddenly and unexpectedly, from unknown causes, during a trip abroad about which many sensational rumors swept the Court. And when his body was brought back to Russia and buried at

Tsarskoe Selo, Anya and the Tsarina regularly visited his premature grave. Together, diligently and tenderly, they returned time and time again to put blankets of fresh and living flowers on the grave where lay buried the historic mystery of that unsolved and highly unusual human relationship.

FAMILY LIFE OF THE IMPERIAL COUPLE

THE BIRTH OF THE HEIR

What was the personal mutual relationship between the Tsar and his wife?

The young Tsarina doubtlessly loved her husband, loved him strongly, sincerely. She was wholly devoted to him. And Nicholas returned this feeling completely.

True, there were differences in the nuances of their mutual love, "I dream of kisses which last forever. Love is eternal—its kisses must burn on my face." Thus, with exalted pathos, the young Tsarina expressed her feelings on the margins of Nicholas II's dry, contained journal. Such exaltation, such romanticism was organically alien to the calm, balanced nature of Nicholas II. His conception of life, of family life was of the simplest and most natural.

The family happiness of the Imperial Couple was heightened at the end of the first year by the birth of a daughter, Olga. Three other daughters were born subsequently and their appearance also brought joy to the household. But this joy was not complete. The intimate dream of the Tsar and Tsarina was to have a son—an heir.

How many prayers were elevated to the Throne of the Almighty for the birth of a son! How many Saints were asked for help! And finally, at the very peak of the Russo-Japanese war, this intimate dream came true. On August 12, 1904, Tsarina Alexandra gave birth to the long-awaited boy. Joy was boundless, all sadness forgotten. The specter of military reverses, internal strife, all was softened by this joyful family occurrence. In those difficult political days the child heir brought the only consolation. A new, broad pageant of life arose before the Sovereigns.

But suddenly it became clear that even this flash of happiness would be poisoned. The infant heir was suffering from an incurable disease—hemophilia. (This hereditary disease is transmitted to children of the male sex through their mothers. The least cut or bruise reduces unstoppable hemorrhages that may bring on the death of the patient.)

The Tsarina knew only too well about this disease—her uncle, her brother, her two nephews had died of it. So much had been said and whispered in her family circles at Darmstadt about this mysterious, nightmarish illness. Why was fate so pitiless towards her? Why did her son, the most precious being on earth to her mother's heart, have to be stricken by that scourge? The bony claws of death will stalk him, follow him step by step, poison his games, perhaps soon they will tear him irreparably away from her motherly arms.

From that moment the whole life of Tsarina Alexandra changed, becoming full of a constant apprehension. Everything else lost its importance. Even the external, gaudy life of the Palace changed. It assumed a new, sterner aspect. Feasts and celebrations of all sorts were avoided, limited to the absolute necessity. Little by little the Imperial Family isolated itself from its entourage, became locked within its own circle.

The frightful disease became the last and decisive turning point in the destiny of Imperial Russia. It ruled the whole latter part of Nicholas II's reign.

But there is no time to lose. One must struggle. At all costs the heir must be saved. Is it possible that science may be powerless? Medicine has made such progress! Science must know and be able to find these means for salvation. All physicians, all specialists available are summoned... they attempt all possible cures... but in vain.

And when Tsarina Alexandra understood that she, the mother, could expect nothing from human beings and from science, she put all her trust and all her hopes in God. He alone can work a miracle. The Sacred Scriptures are explicit on this point. And she throws herself into prayer with all the power of her passionate nature.

Meanwhile, the intervals between attacks of the illness were at times quite lengthy. The child revived, forgot his suffering, engaged in games and was cheerful. How difficult it was to believe at such moments that a woeful infirmity hung over the beautiful, vivacious youngster.

When at such moments the Tsarina heard his gay voice, saw his face flushed from playing, her soul was filled with a new hope. She was sure that the miracle had taken place—God had heard her prayers.

But then, invariably, came disillusion. Hope waned. A sudden attack of the illness would subject the unfortunate, beautiful child to new suffering, putting him once again under the threat of immediate death.

At such times the Tsarina sat by the boy's bedside. She caressed him, kissed his face, his eyes, surrounded him with all kinds of minute cares, attempted to distract him. And in his moments of leisure the Tsar too came into his son's room, bent over his bed and kissed him. With their parental tenderness they hoped to lighten the sufferings of the innocent child who was carrying within himself the scourge of a race.

The despair, the torment of the helpless mother was immeasurably great—for he knew that she herself was the cause of all that misery. And her most passionate prayers did not bring the manifestation of Almighty God's grace which she awaited day and night.

And then, at exactly a similar moment, the crowned mother was confronted by a common Siberian peasant who, in the simple but loud and sure voice of the Russian steppes, told her that which no one had told her before: "Your son will live! Believe in the power of my prayers, believe in the power of my interceding!"

The name of this extraordinary man, dressed in peasant garb with boots and a shirt, was Grigori Rasputin.

And the mother avidly grabbed at the newly rising hope. With all the strength of her soul she believed in the uncommon power of this man who had come forth from the very core of the Russian people. She began to believe that the fate of her child depended from that man and from him alone, just as she had always believed in her imagination that the salvation of Russia and of her Dynasty would come from none other than the people.

RASPUTIN

The village of Pokrovskoe is situated in the middle of the marshes that stretch along the banks of the river Tobola, not far from the city of Tobolsk, on the edge of Western Siberia. Grigori Rasputin was born in that village in the year 1871.

His father's name was Yefim. He did not have a surname, as was often the custom among peasants of that time. The villagers had given him the nickname Novy (New One) for he was not a native of the village.

Many people in Siberia were in the habit of renting out horses to travelers and of going along as coachmen or guides. Yefim, and later his son Grigori, made a living by following that trade. But Grigori was not satisfied with the meager receipts and from early adolescence began to resort to various stratagems to bolster his income, always alert, always ready to seize an opportunity. He was soon suspected in petty thievery and horse stealing. At the same time he began to stand out for his dissoluteness, his nocturnal adventures, his debauchery.

Popular fame tagged him with the nickname of "Rasputin"—meaning in Russian, the depraved one. And from then on this nickname actually became his family name.

One day it happened that this Grigori Rasputin had to serve as coachman to a priest on a trip to the Verkhoturski monastery. The priest, a man with a great reputation for spiritual gifts, fell to talking with Grigori during the trip and was impressed by the peasant's natural talents and by the alertness of his mind. Having drawn him out to a frank admission of his dark, depraved life, the experienced spiritual leader began to exhort the peasant and managed to produce a profound impression on his mind.

Rasputin abandoned his debauches and himself went to the Verkhoturski monastery where for a long time he kept in contact with the monks, listened to the reading of Sacred Scriptures, meditated on their meaning and entered into deep discussions with his new teachers. Later he visited other monasteries as well.

Possessing a tremendous memory and an extremely lively intelligence, Rasputin easily picked up and assimilated everything that he heard. When finally he returned to his native village, its inhabitants did not recognize the old Grigori, whom they remembered for his depraved deeds, in the new, stern, concentrated man who now stood before them.

With deep attention and with interest the peasants of Pokrovskoe and of neighboring villages began to listen to his sermons, delivered in simple, understandable, but weighty words. The people began to talk about his prophecies, his exorcisms and even miracles. And no one around Tobolsk had any doubt left concerning his phenomenal power of suggestion.

***

Those were the days of the political campaigns for the election of the newly instituted State Duma. Father Vostorgov, a priest, was dispatched by the ultra-monarchist organization "Alliance of the Russian People" on a tour of Russian villages to preach the principles of monarchy among the simple people.

Vostorgov was staunchly supported by the government. Local authorities knew about this fact and they met the important priest from the capital with reverence, arranged full attendance at his sermons and were usually even present themselves. As for the ignorant peasants, they listened to the speeches about the Orthodox Faith, autocracy, the people's rights and duties, they nodded their heads and sometimes even muttered, "That's right, Father, that's right…."

Father Vostorgov's job was to send reports to headquarters and pocket traveling money, daily allowances and bonuses.

It was only a matter of time before he reached the village of Pokrovskoe. As usual he began his sermon before the assembled peasants when a highly unusual thing happened—a tall, heavyset man with a beard steps out of the silent crowd and delivers an answering speech.

This was Grigori Rasputin, about whom the traveling priest knew nothing. With simple, clear, but weighty words he rebutted the hazy, obscure and tendentious talk of the priest, producing such an impression on the crowd that, electrified, even unafraid now of the police on duty, it accompanied the official agitator with laughter and jests.

Embarrassed, the local police officer apologized for that "impudent yokel" and even promised to punish him when the occasion arose.

But the experienced and efficient priest did not get angry at Grigori and asked the policeman not to touch him. He had immediately assessed the value of his discovery. "This is the kind of man, the kind of improvised orator from the people that we need for our aims," he thought, noting the name and address of the reformed horse thief.

Having returned to the capital, Father Vostorgov hastened to tell at the very first meeting of the central committee of his Alliance about the impression he had received from a "simple peasant" in the village of Pokrovskoe.

The committee unanimously agreed with the priest's suggestion: Summon Rasputin immediately to the capital to train him for propaganda work among the people in behalf of the Alliance. A sum of money was voted for this purpose.

Local authorities in Siberia received telegrams ordering them to find Rasputin and "deliver" him to the capital. And so, the Tobolsk Police District Inspector Kasimirov, obeying orders, found Rasputin, gave him a government carriage, even police protection, and took him to the nearest railroad station.

There, Captain Katkov, of the railroad police, who also received instructions to furnish Rasputin with a free ticket to Moscow, sensing that this was no ordinary passenger, gave him a whole compartment on the train and assigned a noncommissioned officer to accompany him on the trip.

Neither Inspector Kasimirov, nor Captain Katkov were mistaken in their judgment. Rasputin later remembered them and thanked them with all the largesse of his simple Russian nature.

The train whistle blew. The beat of the wheels on the endless Siberian track began its long and monotonous tattoo under the cars. The trip was to last several days....

A telegram informed Father Vostorgov that his visitor was on the way. But the learned priest was mistaken if he thought that the man coming to him from so far away would soon become an agitator for the Monarchy before the simple Russian folk. The visitor from the wilds was soon to grasp into his hands the destinies of the whole autocratic regime in Russia, was to make his unusual name known all over the world. Here was the representative of the popular lower depths—on his way to meet his Tsar.

What did he, a coarse Siberian peasant, care about the barriers erected by pampered courtiers, by the nobility and bureaucracy between the people and their Tsar? He was a horse thief, he had spent nights and days in the forests and marshes hiding from the law, he was full of the gigantic strength of that black soil he came from.... Those barriers would not be able to stop him. Such was the providential role of the Siberian peasant Rasputin. But at that time it was still hidden from the eyes of everyone.

Least of all did Rasputin himself understand the meaning and the reason for his summons. He was bothered by doubts and misgivings. Could it mean retribution for old sins, for thieving deeds? And he worried about the fate of his wife and children whom he had left at Pokrovskoe. The presence of the railroad policeman in his compartment seemed to corroborate these apprehensions.

However, when the train pulled into the Moscow terminal and Rasputin was cordially greeted by the familiar figure of Father Vostorgov and later, when the priest put him in his private carriage drawn by a well-fed horse and took him to his own home, Rasputin felt reassured. He understood that "it would not be so bad after all."

Rasputin was given new clothes, an embroidered shirt with belt to match, a frock, trousers and knee-high boots and was introduced to the Central Committee of the United Monarchist Organizations in Moscow. The leaders of those organizations were enthusiastic about this "true peasant," this man "endowed with the strength of the black Russian soil."

The crafty, intelligent peasant behaved cautiously at first, mostly kept his peace. He looked around and listened, observed and studied, and drew his conclusions. When he did speak, during that first period, he used laconic, non-committal phrases such as "Why of course," "That is understood," "That's just the way it is," "No use arguing about that."

Only one Monarchist—Attorney P. Bulatsel—dissented from the unanimous approval and frankly expressed his opinion:

"You expect some good from him, but all you are going to get is great harm. I recommend that you immediately liquidate this adventurous project." Bulatsel's suspiciousness and his advice found no echo and did not impair the Monarchists' fascination with Rasputin.

An attempt was made to teach Rasputin manners and delicate speech. But the crafty peasant turned out to be more intelligent and far-seeing than his protectors. He knew that he could never become a dandy and that his best trump lay in his peasant picturesqueness. Observing generally accepted rules of society—don't spit on the floor, don't use the familiar address "thou," don't blow your nose in your napkin and keep your fingernails clean and polished—all this, he knew, would only weaken the down to earth, rough-hewn qualities that he did possess.

He therefore categorically refused to follow any of these precepts.

Father Vostorgov began to initiate him into the mysteries of behind-the-scenes relationships in the high society drawing rooms, and finally it was decided to introduce this man "straight from the people," "straight from the Russian soil" into those very drawing rooms and salons.

From that moment on the broad avenue of success was open for Rasputin.

THE STATE DUMA

The manifesto published by Tsar Nicholas II on October 17, 1905, on one of the most critical days in the revolution of that year, pledged to the Russian people the gift of popular representation in the form of a new elective legislative organ— the State Duma. This act ushered in a new era in the history of the Russian nation.

This basic reform, which greatly circumscribed the monarch's legislative powers, could have given the country a lasting internal peace and prevented any revolution in the future.

In any other country such would doubtlessly have been the case. But the historical pathways of Russia were different. This act of freedom turned out to be "two-faced," just as the complex, retiring soul of Nicholas II, just as the whole destiny of the Russian people. It did not come as a measure duly matured in the consciousness of the Tsar and of his palace retinue, it did not come as an act of evolution in the true sense of the word.

The reform of October 17 had been poisoned even before its birth—poisoned by the wrath and mistrust of the Monarch towards those for whom it was intended. The fruit was picked "green," picked in the midst of raging revolutionary passions, tainted by the fear of some and by the malevolent triumph of others.

And thus, no sooner had the major chords the revolution died down, no sooner had the fires razing the landowners' homes been extinguished and the "red rags" of the demonstrators removed, no sooner had the workers gone back to their jobs and the students to their books and the Court was able to return to the Capital—that the Emperor's soul fell prey to a tormenting drama, to cruel regrets for what he had done.

Russian thought pointed out more than once that the constitutional reform of October 17 had come too late. Had it been granted during the reign of Alexander II together with the other reforms of that liberal Monarch, it would have been historically logical, politically beneficial. The constitutional awareness of Emperor Alexander II was of course deeper and more sincere than that of his grandson Nicholas, just as the whole personality of Alexander, as well as of his collaborators, was more wholesome and more heroic.

But whose fault was it if on the fatal day of March 1, 1881, an act of terrorism killed the best of all Russian monarchs? The constitutional fruit, which had ripened in the 1880s, was trampled to death by a handful of anarchists-fanatics.

Tsar Nicholas II, on the other hand, was unable to rise to a level of reconciliation with destiny whereby he, an absolute Monarch, had been deprived of even a particle of his autocratic power. He was unable to do so to the very end of his days. Moreover, he harbored deep within himself a hatred for everything and everybody in one way or another connected with the day of October 17. He considered that day a day of weakness. And hence came his implacable hatred for Count Witte, the creator of the new regime in Russia.

However, it was impossible to attempt a restoration of absolute power, an annulment of the manifesto. It was even inconceivable to give it the character of a "lost document." And so…. on April 27, 1906, the State Duma was inaugurated. On that day absolutism had to ratify the act of October 17 by means of a general declaration announcing the birth and baptism of a new representational regime.

An extraordinary animation reigned in the Capital. Inside the Palace preparations were made to receive the representatives of the people from all corners of the Russian Empire. Worry and apprehension prevailed here. In the throne hall Empress Alexandra herself personally arranged the ermine cape on which the Tsar was to sit. Her feminine intuition told her that this new breed of people coming from far and wide was not carrying with it a blind devotion and love for the Monarchy.

At the hour appointed for the reception at the Winter Palace, the Deputies picked their way on foot to the palace doors through the curious city crowds that had filled all the surrounding streets. These men were dressed simply, in provincial clothes, some of them wearing peasant's boots and undervests, others still the high-collared shirts of factory workers. They were accompanied by ecstatic shouts of welcome from the crowd. Many onlookers fought back tears and crossing themselves said: "Here are the people coming." And others added: "The people are coming in anger!" A sullen silence from the crowd greeted the passage of the Senators and other dignitaries in their carriages, dressed in glittering uniforms richly embroidered in gold.

The throne hall presented a grandiose spectacle. The whole palace and bureaucratic world of the monarchy was gathered here, gorgeously bedecked, as if purposefully attempting to eclipse the gray and unimpressive aspect of the people's representatives.

Nicholas II entered the Throne Hall with the Empress. There followed a religious service. The Tsar's face did not betray any emotion. His habit of always being exposed to public scrutiny helped the Monarch not to betray the feeling of alarm that gripped him as he came forth to greet those individuals who had gathered there as living symbols of the unrest of the times.

After the religious service the Tsar mounted the steps of the throne and taking a paper from Count Fredericks, the Court Minister, read his speech in a loud and clear voice. This was the first direct address of the Tsar to the Deputies of the First Russian Parliament, in its content it was a purely welcoming speech underlining the divine power of the Monarchy but....

mentioning not a word about the pressing problems in the lives of the Russian people, problems which the Deputies had come here to solve.

Without any previous agreement and without thinking about consequences, the representatives of the people answered the speech with a sullen silence—not a single handclap, no other form of approval. From the height of the throne this was especially noticeable and neither the efforts of the claque in the audience, nor the "hurrahs" of the courtiers, nor the senile chatter of the senators could wipe out the impression created by the unexpected "scandal." On the royal podium all faces seemed frozen in astonishment. Nicholas left the hall. The reception was over. In comparison with the animation that reigned in the streets of the Capital, the Winter Palace looked like an isolated, abandoned spot.

On the following day the State Duma began its legislative work. The first item on its agenda was the compilation of an address to the Monarch. In this document the Duma demanded a radical solution of the fundamental problems of Russian life, first of all of the agrarian problem which concerned a mass of 100 million peasants who expected to see their land lots increased at the expense of state and private holdings. The Duma also demanded an amnesty for political prisoners and a new cabinet of ministers chosen among persons enjoying the trust of Parliament.

The head of the government at the time was ageing Prime Minister I. L. Goremykin. The Tsar had named him to that post a few days before the opening of the flume. At the same time he had named the Governor of the Saratov district,

Stolypin, to the post of Minister of the Interior.

Goremykin did not represent any definite political trend. This dyed-in-the-wool bureaucrat once said about himself: "You know, they took me out of moth balls!" The Tsar made an historical mistake when he entrusted the solution of such a vital problem as the practical application of the idea of popular representation to individuals who themselves did not approve of this idea, had struggled against it all their lives and were used to build worshipful altars to absolutism. (When Emperor Alexander I dreamed about freedom he turned to Count Speransky, well known for his liberal attitudes. Alexander II entrusted the executing of his liberating reforms to Count Rostovtsev, Miliutin and finally to Count Loris-Melikov.)

How can one be surprised that an immediate conflict arose between Goremykin's cabinet and the first people's representative body. This conflict reached a particularly acute stage on the day when Prime Minister Goremykin in answer to the Duma's address rejected the possibility of carrying out the reforms demanded by Parliament.

Shouts of anger, whistles and cries of "Resignation! Resignation!" broke out in the chamber. After this event the Premier could not make another personal appearance at the Duma. Such an abnormal situation of course could not last very long. The Tsar was confronted by two alternatives: either dismiss the Duma, or form a new cabinet with liberal members of the Duma itself.

The Supreme Council, under the chairmanship of the Tsar, called in session especially to solve this paramount question, voted overwhelmingly for the second alternative. Only two men stood for the dismissal of the Duma. These were I. L. Goremykin and the new Minister of the Interior. No one among those present had any doubts that the Tsar himself was inclined to submit to the will of the majority. And yet, facts proved to be quite different. Here is what transpired behind the thick curtain of palace secrecy that hid the peculiarities of Nicholas II's nature and the motives of his sovereign acts from the eyes of contemporaries.

At the end of that historical meeting the Tsar asked the Premier to wait and when they were left alone he spoke in the following words: "Well, Ivan Loginovich, you and I were defeated." "Your Majesty," answered Premier Goremykin, "Even now your absolute power can decide matters one way or the other. Personally, my opinion is still the same!"

The Tsar thought for a minute, wiped his mustache with a characteristic gesture of the hand and then, crossing himself, said: "Well then, let it be your way, Ivan Loginovich!"

The Premier immediately went to the printing office of the State Council and personally supervised the printing of the Tsar's directive for the dismissal of the Duma. This directive was to appear on the following morning. Possessing a purely Olympian calm, a product of many years of bureaucratic service, the ageing Premier returned home as if nothing had occurred, had supper, smoked his customary cigar and went to bed.

Meanwhile Tsar Nicholas had had time to think matters over and to change his mind. Around midnight a messenger of the Tsar went to Goremykin with a new order: "Do not dismiss the Duma!"

What was the Premier's reaction? As if the evil fate of the Russian land were calling the moves on that night, Goremykin did not receive the messenger under the pretext that he was resting and that the Tsar's orders would be carried out upon his awakening.

Nicholas II's astonishment knew no bounds when on the following morning he learned that the Imperial directive about the dismissal of the Duma had already been published. Goremykin himself immediately went to Tsarskoe Selo and presented to the Monarch his most humble apologies. At the same time he asked to be permitted to resign. The Tsar accepted his resignation and named the Minister for the Interior, P. A. Stolypin, in his stead.

The new Premier was undoubtedly an outstanding man, extremely energetic and resolute. He had shown these qualities in his struggle against all manifestation of terrorism and banditism which from the days of the 1905 revolution were still rampant all over Russia. His sharp and unequivocal actions brought a measure of tranquility to the land. This fact immediately raised Stolypin's prestige in the eyes of the Monarch.

Stolypin showed a similar determination in his dealings with the young Russian Parliament. When after the dismissal of the First Duma the Second Duma turned out to be just as opposed the Government, Premier Stolypin did not hesitate to obtain from the Monarch not only its dismissal but also some changes in the electoral laws whereby the number of deputies from the central and traditionally conservative provinces could be increased at the expense of the representation of border provinces and other opposition-minded areas.

His plan worked: the Third Duma, elected according to the new laws turned out in its majority to be favorable to the Government. This was Stolypin's triumph. His prestige reached its zenith. Finally, it seemed, the long-awaited peace had come to stay in the country.

That was an interesting page in the history of Tsarism, the last flash exalting the "old regime." Stolypin did not consider the idea of the "old world" as finished. He still believed in its vitality, in the possibility of revitalizing it even further, in the possibility of "pouring new wine into old skins."

Here are the famous words he once threw at an opposition and socialistically minded group of deputies of the Second Duma: "You need great upheavals, I need a great Russia!" These words, uttered boldly and masterfully, rolled all over Russia like thunder and hurt the opposition to the quick. Had the all-powerful Premier taken advantage of the calm reigning in the country at the time to carry out a radical agrarian reform, giving land to the multi-million peasant mass, as the First State Duma had requested, then the ghost of revolution would have been pushed away for a long, long time.

One of the chieftains of Bolshevism, Leon Trotsky, candidly declared: "We never could have seized power, had the peasantry been given land in time."

Of course Stolypin understood the role of the agrarian question in the future destiny of Russia; presumably he also understood that the old regime could hardly continue existing by inertia alone. But Stolypin did not dare to infringe upon the interests of great land holders. This would have offended not only the average landowner, but the state treasury as well, and especially the court aristocracy.

The agrarian reform which Stolypin did undertake and which consisted in distributing the communal land for private ownership by the peasants did not substantially improve the lot of the Russian peasantry; in practice it only modified the ownership title, without increasing the holdings of any individual family.

In these years Stolypin could have saved, but.... did not save the old regime. He could have become a Minin, a Pozharsky. Instead, he became only an episode, brilliant it's true, but still only an episode in that troubled period of Russian history. [Minin and Pozharsky: In the "Time of Troubles" (1611–13) when various bands of invaders (Poles, Cossacks, insurgents and plain marauders) were ravaging the Russian land, there arose two men—Minin, a simple merchant, and Prince Pozharsky, a noble and prominent military figure. They collected money and organized an army which finally cleared Russia of all invaders and marauders, thus paving the way for the election of the first Romanov Tsar.]

Eventually, Stolypin was not able alas, to avoid the fate of all major statesmen during Nicholas II's reign. Men of stature bothered and embarrassed the Monarch, with them he did not feel at ease. Like Count Witte before him, Stolypin fell into disgrace and lost his influence at court. Besides, by that time there seemed to be no further need for a strong pacifier in the land!

If Stolypin was never formally sent into retirement, it was only because here again the odd destiny of Russia intervened and played a decisive hand. Unexpectedly, out of a clear blue sky, Stolypin was shot in a theatre in the city of Kiev at a gala performance in the presence of the Emperor, shot from a service revolver by a secret police agent named Bogrov.

While Stolypin lay dying from a wound in his liver, the Emperor came to the hospital to visit him. Leaving the room, the Tsar turned to his companions and said, "Imagine! Madame Stolypina just told me that there still are Susanins in the Russian land, and that her husband, like Susanin, is dying for me! That's a little too much, don't you think?"

Stolypin's wife had mentioned Susanin (a peasant hero who in 1613 sacrificed his life for the first Romanov by leading the invading Poles away from the Tsar's hiding place) because by that time it had already become known that the Premier's assassin had been admitted to the theatre with the knowledge of Stolypin's collaborator, Chief of Police Kurlov. The story of a twentieth century Susanin, however, soon paled and lost its sharpness in the tense atmosphere of that political moment when all of Russia was shocked by such an enigmatic assassination.

Tsar Nicholas named a special commission, headed by Senator Trusevich, once Director of the Police Department, with specific orders to conduct an exhaustive investigation of the murder. The findings of the investigation, however, amounting to thirty large volumes, were never made public, and were kept in a special metal cabinet in the secret Senate Archive. The Soviet Government later considered it necessary to transfer these documents to the Moscow Archive Museum, where they are now kept in the secret section.

But there is no such mystery that sooner or later will not be pierced by a ray of light. Here is the solution of that particular historic enigma.

Stolypin's assassin, Dimitri Bogrov by name, son of a wealthy house owner in Kiev, turned out to be a convinced and "sincere" revolutionary anarchist. Thus he defined himself in a letter to his family on September 10, 1911, on the eve of his execution. At the same time, ever since 1907, Bogrov had been serving in the Kiev secret police, the "Okhrana," which in this particular case used him for its mysterious purposes. The "Okhrana," it became known later, had promised Bogrov to help him flee the theatre after his deed. Immediately after the assassination, they told him, all lights in the theatre would go out and he would be able to slip through an open door into the hall where he would find a military coat and a cap; from there he would rush to the street where an automobile would be waiting for him to carry him away.

This is why, having fired the revolver, Bogrov remained on the spot, wasting precious seconds, waiting for the promised darkness. But this darkness did not materialize. Why? It so happened that the mechanic on duty by the switch box refused to allow the member of the "Okhrana" to come near the box, in spite of the fact that the latter had with him and presented a police identification badge. Thus the plan for Bogrov's rescue collapsed! (Twenty years later the authenticity of this information, gathered by the author during his service with the Imperial Senate, was fully corroborated by A. F. Ghirs, Governor of the Kiev District at the time of the historic assassination, in a speech made in Paris on October 26, 1931, at a meeting organized in memory of P. Stolypin.)

But what were Bogrov's personal motives in this matter? "Revenge for the Jews!" he answered during the interrogation conducted by the Chief of the Kiev "Okhrana," Colonel Kuliabko, under orders from Senator Trusevich. Bogrov considered Stolypin an enemy of the Jews. This fact was confirmed during interrogations by his brother, V. Bogrov. To the question why hadn't he shot the Tsar who was sitting so near to Stolypin, Bogrov answered: "Such a sensational murder could have provoked strong repressions and pogroms! Besides, Nicholas is only a toy in Stolypin's hands. No, it was best to kill Stolypin."

When the future historian will say his final, unbiased word about Premier Stolypin, he will also have to answer the following question: What were the motives of the Tsar's "Okhrana" hierarchy when they directed the hand of the Anarchist Bogrov against the last outstanding statesman of Imperial Russia?

The fatal destiny of Russia found a vivid reflection in the fate of Peter Stolypin.

When Tsar Alexander III died, the German Emperor Wilhelm II doubtlessly felt relieved: fate had removed a neighbor famous for his immovable firmness. Deep down in his soul the Kaiser was convinced that he would easily assume the role of patron and mentor of the young Tsar Nicholas II about whose weakness of character he knew only too well. Such a conviction must have been further strengthened by the German origin of the young Tsarina Alexandra.

Meanwhile, that was an historical epoch when the political

horizons of Europe were by no means free from menacing clouds. The Franco-Russian alliance had not yet acquired its stability. Relations between Russia and Germany remained undefined. The political accord engineered by the Iron Chancellor Bismarck and Tsar Alexander III no longer existed, nor was there any trace left of the beneficial influence towards peace preservation which had been exercised by these two statesmen now gone from the arena of history.

The Franco-Russian rapprochement, it is true, did not disrupt the traditional friendly relations between Russia and Germany. The Russian Minister for Foreign Affairs Girs, and after him Count Lansdorf, remained too faithful to the ideologies the old, classical school of diplomacy to risk wrecking this relationship. And Wilhelm II, well remembering the legacy of his grandfather who had built his whole foreign policy on a close friendship with Russia, wanted to keep things as they were.

Lacking a formal alliance, the vacuum in Russo-German relations had to be filled by the traditional and purely dynastic closeness between the Russian and German Imperial houses. Obviously, the personal mutual attitude of the two crowned neighbors thus assumed the form of a very important political factor in preserving peaceful relations between the two most powerful countries in the Europe of that tine.

Were the two monarchs endowed, in their characters and temperaments, with the essential qualities whereby, in guiding the destinies of their people, they could preserve a stable and lengthy peace between the two nations? Time, swiftly moving, was already preparing an answer to this searching question.

The first personal meeting between Tsar Nicholas II and Kaiser Wilhelm took place in the city of Breslau. It is doubtful whether this occasion helped to promote friendship between the two monarchs. As it turned out, before his trip to Breslau, the young Tsar decided to visit Vienna, allegedly as a token of special attention towards the ageing Austrian Emperor Franz Joseph. The Tsar did this on the advice of the Minister of Foreign Affairs, Prince Labanov Rostovski, who, even though a proponent of friendly relations with Berlin, had little personal liking for the Kaiser.

Meanwhile, a few days prior to the Tsar's arrival in Germany, it became known that photographs had appeared in Berlin, showing both Emperors together, the Kaiser two heads taller than the Russian Tsar, patronizingly embracing his crowned guest. When he became aware of this Nicholas II was extremely displeased and ordered his embassy to buy and eliminate the whole stock of these photos.

A military review was organized in honor of the Russian Tsar. Nicholas II appeared in the Prussian uniform of the Badenberg Hussars, a regiment of which he was honorary commander. Wilhelm II also wore a Prussian uniform, but... had chosen not to wear the sash of Andrei Pervosvanny, the highest decoration in Russia, of which he was a bearer. Throughout the review the Kaiser kept spurring his mount in an effort to keep constantly ahead of his guest. This maneuver did not escape Nicholas and he, an excellent rider, responded in the same fashion. As a result, the two Emperors finished the review at an unseemly rapid pace, almost at a trot!

A solemn dinner was held in honor of the Russian crowned

guest. The Kaiser and the Tsar exchanged friendly speeches of greeting and the Kaiser's address sounded particularly enthusiastic when he underscored the mutual warm feelings existing between the two monarchs, based on a family relationship.

Still, this first meeting on the whole left a rather unpleasant impression in the Tsar's mind. This fact came clearly into view in the following year when the Russian Imperial couple decided to pay a visit to the Tsarina's birthplace, modest, old-fashioned Darmstadt. They did not go there via Berlin, but followed an itinerary skirting the German Capital. They did this to avoid a meeting with Wilhelm.

The Kaiser was displeased and told so to the Russian Ambassador, Count Osten Saken. The German Emperor's displeasure would have left no lasting trace, however, had not Tsar Nicholas repeated the same motion on the following year. This time the Kaiser was seriously incensed and gave free rein to his temperament. This happened at an official dinner given by Admiral General Prince Heinrich, brother of the Kaiser.

After dinner the Kaiser lit a cigar and invited Count Osten Saken and the Imperial Chancellor, Prince Bulow, to follow him. The talk immediately assumed an hostile character. The Kaiser delivered himself of harsh reproaches against Nicholas II and allegations that he, the Kaiser, was not appreciated in Russia according to his merits. The Kaiser finally reached a point where he wrathfully exclaimed: "The continuation of a similar conduct will lead Russia to the most serious consequences!"

These words were equivalent to a threat of severing Russo-

German relations. Count Osten Saken, who as Russian representative was the target of all these words, maintained an unshakeable and dignified calm. He let the Kaiser have his say and even then remained silent until finally the Kaiser himself asked him what refutation he could present.

At this point, with a smile on his face, the Count answered: "Very little, Your Majesty! I am convinced you don't believe yourself in what you just told me, and even less can you do anything about it. You know very well that you need Russia more than we need Germany!" Then the Count reminded Wilhelm of the friendly Russian neutrality during the Franco-Prussian war, a position that had insured Germany's victory.

Noticing how the Kaiser's face gradually lost its somber expression, the Russian ambassador switched the conversation to historical anecdotes with his usual masterfulness and half an hour later there remained no trace of the German ruler's ominous mood. Persons sitting in the adjoining room heard bursts of laughter and later, when time came to take leave, Wilhelm II shook the Ambassador's hand and thanked him with obvious sincerity for a pleasant evening.

In spite of the political insignificance of this episode, it is still highly characteristic, showing as it does clearly all the impulsiveness in Wilhelm II's character, an impulsiveness that could so suddenly and sharply change the moods of the man who ruled the destinies of the German nation.

And this unusual talk between a monarch and an accredited ambassador did have its consequences. Tsar Nicholas decided to visit the Kaiser on his way back to Russia and stopped for a day in Potsdam. This meeting was characterized by a rather intimate family atmosphere and was not marked by any official pomp. At dinner the Kaiser made a short, purely welcoming speech. The departure of the Russian sovereign couple was scheduled for 10 p.m. that same evening.

The Russian Tsarina arrived to the station in the company of Countess Brockdorf, the Oberhofmeisterin of the Kaiser's Court. The two Monarchs followed the Tsarina. But the German Empress was conspicuous only by her absence. Her excuse had been that she had to be ready in half an hour to meet the Swedish Crown Prince and his spouse. The Tsar was furious. "What an unheard of impertinence," he fumed, speaking into the ear of Count Osten Saken. "To send the Empress to the station with that Brockdorf woman!"

Don't similar occurrences bear witness that even those who hold in their hands the fate of their people are subject to all the minute human weaknesses, just as ordinary mortals?

It is really astonishing how dissimilar these two contemporary monarchs were in their characters. Kaiser Wilhelm II, full of conceit, vanity and confidence in his own omnipotence appears as the direct opposite of the modest, timid and delicate young Russian Emperor. Nicholas II was selfishly vain in his own way—he could stand much, for example, that his father, Alexander III, would never have tolerated, but on the other hand he was incensed by things to which his father would not have paid the slightest attention. Alexander III had been vain as a Tsar, but simple and modest in his personal life.

The Kaiser's vanity was of a different kind. He was unrecognizable in questions of political importance. When the interests of his Reich required it, he was able to forget all the cheapness of human vanity. He employed all means, for example, including favor-currying, to gain Nicholas II's good graces, and then… the German Emperor would always take the return match with a vengeance! For this the Kaiser liked to take advantage of personal interviews, purposefully giving them an intimate character. Tsar Nicholas, soft and thoughtful, was unable to withstand the Kaiser's craftiness and gave in each time. Russian diplomacy and the interests of the Russian nation always lost in similar conditions.

For example, it was precisely by such a maneuver that the Kaiser was able to occupy the strategically important Bay of Kio-Chao.

The Russian Tsar did not like people like Wilhelm II. With them he felt ill at ease. They seemed to shock him by their activeness, poses, gestures and by their "satanic" will power. The Kaiser in particular had a depressing effect upon Nicholas II by means of the complexity of his Prussian military apparatus, of the methodical preparedness of his staffs, completely ready for warfare.

In this vast game, played between the two Emperors on a grandiose international arena, Russian diplomacy always had to be on the alert, applying all its mastery to prevent this game from infringing upon the interests of the Russian nation. Count Osten Saken, more than anyone else had to carry the brunt of this difficult role and tread the slippery ground of Berlin diplomatic circles.

Just as his predecessor, Count Shuvalov, he was an outstanding ambassador, a diplomat of the old conservative school. Thanks to an innate social sense, a dignified self-control and a cool and profound intelligence he was able to maneuver successfully between Berlin and the Russian Court. More than once was he called upon to extinguish the sparks that flew so often, threatening to set off a conflagration, thanks to the Kaiser's incontinence and the lack of character and mutability of the Russian Monarch.

The Count knew Wilhelm's complex character to perfection, he studied his weaknesses. In the Count's evaluation Wilhelm II was an outstanding man, but always a man who under the influence of the moment was equally capable of generous impulses and of less laudable actions. Likewise, under the influence of a moment he could make decisions of great political importance. And yet, there was no stubbornness in him. With a certain adroitness, taking advantage of a propitious time it was comparatively easy to guide this way or that the ruler who once had written in the Munich golden book: "Sic volo—sic jubeo." (As I wish, so I command.)

And the Count knew quite well how to talk to the Kaiser. It is not at all surprising then that the Russian diplomat enjoyed a tremendous prestige and influence in Berlin. Wilhelm often, and sometimes without warning, visited the Russian Embassy where he would tarry for prolonged conversations on political themes of the day.

Countess Osten Saken was an invaluable helpmate to her husband. An accomplished musician, Chopin's pupil in her youth, she knew how to create an atmosphere of social coziness. In meeting her, Emperor Wilhelm would kiss her hand as a sign of special respect.

Who knows—would the Kaiser have so lightly smothered Serbian independence with his German shield, would he have overstepped the danger signal that stood on the border between peace and war, if Count Osten Saken had been occupying the post of Russian Ambassador in Berlin during those critical summer days in 1914, preceding the outbreak of World War I?

CODA

[Editor's note: This tribute by Michael N. Kalantar appeared in *American Slav Magazine*, March, 1942]

To the Memory of General K. I. Globochev

A notice appeared recently in the Russian newspapers of New York City, of the death, in this city, of Major-General K. I. Globochev, who occupied the post of the chief of the Petrograd Secret police [St. Petersburg "Okhrana"] in the era of the wane of Tsarism.

General Globochev had died suddenly, of a heart attack. The newspapers said that on the eve of his death he was in good health, had gone out, had played with his grandchildren. Next morning, however, he had been taken ill and…half an hour later, alas, he was dead.

An impartial observer, who was a participant in the events which brought the downfall of Tsarism, can hardly pass by the fresh grave without paying tribute to the qualities of this astute and powerful police official who had rendered valuable services to the regime to which he had devoted all his energies.

Not one of those who surrounded the Russian Throne had felt as acutely as did General Globochev the heavy tread of the impending revolution. The daily reports of the chief of the Gendarmery painted an almost exhaustive picture of the approaching collapse and of the ominous, threatening danger.

In fact, from the very beginning of January 1917, the Secret police reports to the Russian monarch spoke again and again of the sinister symptoms—the disorganization of the food supply, the growing discontent of the masses, the successful spreading of revolutionary underground activities and even the menace of hunger riots.

"Events of extreme importance pregnant with serious consequences are certainly near at hand" said the report of January 28th.

When there was talk in the influential government circles of dissolving the Duma, the wise chief of the Gendarmes, unafraid of the wrath of his superiors, warned the Tsar that should such a measure be carried out the government would have to deal not with the deputies alone, but…with the entire Russian people.

With the accuracy of a seismograph the Secret police reports noted the approaching earthquake. In his "strictly confidential" report of February 5th, Globochev foresaw the events which were to take place exactly two weeks later:

"The bitter resentment of the people is increasing and there is no end to it in sight; moreover, there can be no doubt that once the fury of the masses are released, acts of incredible cruelty and brutality will mark the beginning of a most terrible revolution."

But alas, the destiny of the Russian Monarchy was already written down in the book of fate and nothing could avert its doom—even such apparently authoritative sources of information as the Secret police reports had been in vain.

These reports were also read by the Minister of the Interior, Protopopov—and calmly shelved. The administration interpreted the situation in its own way. Minister Protopopov had his private plans about saving the Empire. He believed in his horoscope. Belonging to the inner, occult circle of the Tsarina, he assured those present that he was born under the sign of Jupiter, which is subordinated to Saturn and therefore...invested with the confidence of his monarch, he was invincible.

The chief of the Secret police, however, knowing every minute secret of the palace's private life, understood the hopelessness of the situation; yet, duty bound, he would not desert his post in time of peril, but was prepared to face it.

"The Gendarmery, entrusted to me," said his last report, "will of course, bend all its strength to fight the revolution, though, I am afraid, this strength will not be sufficient to cope with the elemental fury of the masses."

The governmental ship was then on the road to destruction!

***

The grandiose settings of the Imperial might had collapsed! Now came a dull succession of painful days in exile, days no longer filled with the strain of maintaining order within the sixth part of the globe, but with the everyday worries of personal life. But characters of high caliber do not lose their dignity even in the most adverse circumstances.

Thus, to the end of his days General Globochev was true to the precepts which he had served so faithfully. He had not repudiated them for the new modern life he was obliged to lead.

Many intimate secrets of the Imperial Court had been confided to General Globochev—secrets for which the sensation loving public is so avid. However, the high police official had not succumbed to temptation, but had firmly kept the seal of silence and taken these secrets to his grave.

The venerable veteran of a past era has ended his days, across the ocean, in a distant foreign land, yet he had been able to lighten his exile by finding happiness within the circle of his family—did not the newspapers' notice say that on the eve of his death he was in good health, had gone out, had played with his grandchildren?

"Sic tibi terra levis"—May the earth rest light upon you.

M. N. Kalantar, L.L.D.

APPENDIX
INTERVIEW WITH LEO TOLSTOY

[Editor's note: This article was written circa 1950 during the height of the Red Scare, when Joseph Stalin's political aggression was a pressing concern in the U.S.]

RUSSIA'S PROBLEM

By Dr. Michael N. Kalantar
Expert of International Law and History
Author and Journalist. Graduate of
the Universities of Heidelberg (Germany)
Sorbonne (France) and Petrograd (Russia)

In these dark days with humanity shuddering over the menace and potentialities of the atom bomb, a vivid picture comes to mind focusing upon my last meeting with the great Russian writer and humanist, Count Leo Tolstoy. A book which I had written [had] just been published and the Count was interested in it as it dealt with the characteristics of governmental and cultural currents in contemporary Russia. He asked that I come to his estate at Yasnaya Polyana to discuss the work with him.

I found the venerable author in a most genial mood. Apparently he awaited my arrival with some impatience. "This is a happy day!" he exclaimed, somewhat agitated, but stressing each word with a singular emphasis. He waved a current copy of a Moscow newspaper. "I've only just read in this newspaper that yesterday in Moscow there was a postponement for the third time in carrying out of a death sentence, all because, mind you! that for no amount of money could an executioner be found! It will now be necessary to import one from Petersburg. Think of it! That means that in all of Russia it is impossible to find two executioners!"

Tempora mutantur! How times do change! How bitterly ironic sound these profound words of the great humanist in these Stalinist days.

Tolstoy lived within the rich and deep traditions of the nineteenth century. Although the passing years have accumulated into the twentieth century, Russia and the world have sadly retrogressed as the years have advanced. Ours is an infinitely less happy era from any point of view, whether moral, emotional or political. He was not familiar with such exercise of despotic power over men, such disunity and distrust of nations. At one time moral principles were the foundation upon which was built the structure of international law. Of course the past century was not without its sins and errors, but those who lived its years at least escaped the horrors of concentration camps, the tortures of innocent people, the shooting of guiltless hostages, the seizure and wanton persecution of entire nations or the cruel liquidation of whole classes—priests, farmers—and the destruction of religious faith.

How did Mankind arrive at the brink of chaos in the contemporary crisis? Where are the springs that feed this river of universal misfortune? How can humanity insure itself from annihilation by the atomic menace? These questions are put to me more and more each passing day. I endeavor to answer them calling upon my experience and knowledge of history and international law.

Glancing backward into the not too distant past and examining with historical perspective of events, it is not difficult to detect the political errors which the West has made in the complacent years between the two World Wars. It is these errors and political blunders that spawned the growth and rise of both Russian Bolshevism and German Nazism. They permitted Stalin and Hitler to consolidate their new-found strength—they created their military potential. They also gave rise to the fatal relation of forces as they stood on the eve of World War II—to the situation in which the Western democracies found themselves. Confronting us at this moment were two enemies, Hitler and Stalin, Fascism and Communism. The fact that they rivaled each other did not banish or lessen the threatening menace they signified.

Today it is possible to consider as entirely credible the fact that the military alliance between Hitler and Stalin, an alliance which seemed so monstrous to the free world, should have been, according to recent evidence, accomplished on Stalin's initiative rather than by Hitler. It was the Red dictator who in the first place, several months before the war began, suggested to the German Fuehrer an alliance against the Western democracies, while the German partisans of the pact assisted in attempting to have Hitler agree to it.

Stalin was well aware of what he was doing. The witless German dictator had dreams of firing the world. Crafty Stalin handed him the torch calculating that the ensuing war would exhaust the democracies and Hitler alike until Stalin would be given the opportunity of meddling in the bloody clash and with inconsequential losses establish his domination over the world.

The astute plan of the plotting Red Generalissimo did not however succeed. Hitler's pact with Stalin was terminated by the unexpected invasion of Russian territories by German Panzer divisions.

Thus it was by no means of choice or his own initiative that Stalin found himself a bedfellow of the Western democracies. It was Hitler who made Stalin our ally! From the point of view of pure ideology, for the sake of the moral justification of the war, it would have indeed been far better if Stalin had remained in unholy alliance with Hitler against the Western nations. From the military viewpoint however, our alliance with Stalin was a profitable one for us; he made ultimate victory more assured, and we accepted it. Not to accept it was, indeed, out of the question.

In accepting it, the Western democracies yielded to some illusions and made some mistakes. We had forgotten that all the irreconcilable contradictions existing between Stalin's dictatorship and the democratic regime of the West had by no means been lessened or eliminated, but continued in force.

Not for one instant did Stalin forget this. He conducted his own particular and separate war. In other words—bear this in mind—during the entire period of World War II we were dealing with two enemies—one an open enemy, the other a secret one. The political leaders of the West could not observe this. We wished to believe that at the war's conclusion the Stalinist regime would change—that it was accomplishing the will of the people—that the Soviet regime was on the eve of an authentic revolution, and that the victorious Russian people would ultimately prove stronger than their masters and would overwhelm them. Few among us wished to understand that Stalin, far from being concerned with the Allied cause and democratic concepts, was in fact irreconcilably hostile to them. He considered his provisional alliance with democracies as his alliance with Hitler as a springboard to world revolution and that at war's end with Germany fully conquered and prostrate would come the third war, a war which has thus far proved to be a "cold war."

No one seemed to grasp or understand this nor attempt to believe it. Why? Fundamentally because the political leaders of the West wholeheartedly believed in the decency of the Soviets. It is quite impossible to blame them. In fact it only does them honor since only for the decent is it possible to believe in the decency of others. As for the Soviets, they never for a moment believed in decency in international intercourse, nor do they now hold such beliefs or intentions of ever changing.

Realization of shattered illusions came slowly and had not kept apace with events. Our grasping of the full significance of what had happened came only when many positions had already been lost—Romania, Bulgaria, Czechoslovakia, Poland, et al. Fortunately this period may now be considered closed. Another period, a new period has arrived.

As far as it is possible, in a measure, to judge the future from the present, this future is based on three fundamentals— the Truman Doctrine, the Marshall Plan and the Atlantic Pact. These foundations will strengthen with the passage of time. If, according to legend, the ancient world could rest on three whales, why cannot our modern world maintain itself upon these three principles? Our "whales" however, even as those of ancient days, should be of unyielding might—the Truman Doctrine, the Marshall Plan and the Pact. They should be abundant with will, resolution and determination, and carried out by men of high caliber with unshakeable perseverance.

A difference exists between will and desire. It must be remembered that the Communists are hardly lacking in will. Nor is will and desire equally potent or equally valuable. Will is something very powerful; it strengthens the muscles—while mere desire is a weakening thing. Will demands action—desire merely calls to discussion, to dreams and wishes of agreement, of compromise, appeasement. Remember, Bolshevism is a well-oiled organized machine. Its propaganda foams with shameless lies. It has organizations that are both legal and illegal. Its fingers control the push-buttons operating its universal tentacles. A button is pressed and there are strikes in France. Another causes the Red Army invading China to go into action. A third button is pressed and top-secret documents concerning the atom vanish into thin air from the most secure vaults.

On the other hand, does this devil's fabric with its tactics of lies and cunning make Bolshevism something unshakeable and unconquerable? Have ever such roots of falsehood and evil been sources of strength?

There is consolation in the fact that the Red Menace has its weak and vulnerable spots. If it were possible to direct a blow against these weak spots then the current "cold" war would have less chance of being transformed into a "hot" war and it is possible that the Soviet regime would at the beginning be forced into retreat and ultimately destroyed. One of these vulnerable spots is the impasse under whose external guise of Kremlin might, Communism finds itself today in the U.S.S.R. A bottomless abyss exists today between the Soviet masters and the Russian people which is the Achilles heel of the close-knit Red network.

The privileged Kremlin minority is an oligarchy—the Communist Party and the M.V.D.—the secret police. These assuredly are not the Russian people.

The people or peoples of Russia are today in fact the most anti-Communist peoples on earth. They all know, without exception, from the high Party official down to the political prisoner, that the happy land-of-milk-and-honey propaganda is a preposterous lie. One has never heard of a downtrodden person escaping into Russia. The escape route has always been a one-way street—to the West. But those with fettered hands and feet, living under the fears of a terroristic state, who know little truth about the life of peoples on the other side of the Iron Curtain—how can these cry out in the wilderness or raise their heads in revolt?

The United States, heading the coalition of the West, alien to militarism and goals of conquest, has entered the struggle not for gain but only for the survival of the free way of life and the preservation of free institutions in the world. This American concept, should without fail, be transmitted to the peoples on the darkened side of the Iron Curtain; it should be transmitted skillfully, bearing in mind the psychology of the oppressed Soviet masses. By methods of shrewd counter-propaganda, not based on former, now obsolete patterns, we can confuse and confound the shameless game the Communists play and millions of people on the other side of the Dark Curtain will become our authentic allies.

Having strengthened the Atlantic Pact with the signatures of a dozen free nations and having strengthened the forces of the new coalition, we should not lose sight of our most important ally in the coming gigantic struggle—an ally not consisting of a mere group of people, but a nation of 180,000,000 Russians who, more than all others, thirst for freedom and peace.

It is certain that the Russian people in a vast majority will not defend the terroristic regime which oppresses it. They have nothing to defend, not even their home or farms; for nothing in all Russia's vast latitudes belongs to them. It is all Stalin's!

AFTERWORD
by Irene Vartanoff

During and after World War II, it was routine to run an FBI investigation of any naturalized citizens hired to work for the U.S. government in sensitive areas, to establish their loyalty to the U.S. During the standard investigation of Dr. Kalantar, one agent noted that the writings of a potentially suspect organization to which Kalantar belonged, whose members were mostly emigrés displaced by the Russian Revolution, were "politically naive" and thus harmless.

Politically naive? No, say rather, politically hopeful. Thus it is with all lost causes. History eventually passes them by, diminishing them despite the human tragedies enacted. The survivors become a footnote to history.

Anyone interested in reading more about what happened to individuals of the Tsarist-era Russian establishment who remained in their homeland after the Bolsheviks took over should check out *Former People, the Final Days of the Russian Aristocracy* by Douglas Smith. It describes in detail the miseries of that life choice.

For those who escaped, there was a different sort of pain. The relics of the Russian Revolution—as I used to callously call them when I was a teenager—had memories of sweet days gone by. They had vain hopes of correcting what they believed was a huge mistake in the political and social direction of their native land. Dashed hopes, as the years and then the decades went by, and communism seemed firmly entrenched. Then it changed after all, as my father had always predicted, once the original revolutionaries died off. Their fiercely held beliefs no longer ruled Russia, and a new and different Russia, yet still the same Russia, was born again. Tempora mutantur indeed. How times change, and yet Russia remains.